I Have Been

Buried

Under Years

of Dust

Valerie Gilpeer
& Emily Grodin

WILLIAM MORROW

An Imprint of HarperCollins*Publishers*

I Have Been

A MEMOIR

Buried

OF AUTISM

Under Years

AND HOPE

# of Dust

I HAVE BEEN BURIED UNDER YEARS OF DUST. Copyright © 2021 by Emily Faith Grodin and Valerie Gilpeer. All rights reserved. Printed in the United States of America. No part of this book may be used or reproduced in any manner whatsoever without written permission except in the case of brief quotations embodied in critical articles and reviews. For information, address HarperCollins Publishers, 195 Broadway, New York, NY 10007.

HarperCollins books may be purchased for educational, business, or sales promotional use. For information, please email the Special Markets Department at SPsales@harpercollins.com.

FIRST EDITION

Library of Congress Cataloging-in-Publication Data has been applied for.

ISBN 978-0-06-298434-0 (Hardcover)
ISBN 978-0-06-308306-6 (International Edition Paperback)

21 22 23 24 25 LSC 10 9 8 7 6 5 4 3 2 1

*For every person who is searching
for their voice, and all those who struggle to be heard.
We dedicate these words to you.*

—E.G.

Hello readers,

For 25 years I was trapped inside a body without a voice. Through the help of my communication partner, I have learned to type. I'm now able to really express my thoughts and feelings in a way I never thought possible. The years used to pass me by and I was merely an onlooker of my own life. Now I am the one making the decisions about my life and won't ever again be silent. I'm so very grateful every single day. Please friends, do me a real favor and be open minded when you meet someone on the autism spectrum. I can guarantee that there is more to them than you can see.

Sincerely,

Emily

Prologue

"Is this Tom Grodin, father of Emily Grodin?" the woman on the other end of the phone asked my husband. She sounded out of breath and fraught.

Now what? I wondered. Tom and I were settling down for the night, getting ready for bed. That the call was tied to our daughter, Emily, twenty-five, went without saying. We were used to such calls, just not what came next.

"The police are here, seven of them," she said. "Emily's caregiver has been hurt and she needs to go to the ER. I'm not sure exactly what happened, but apparently Emily got aggressive and now there's a lot of commotion. She's very upset. I need you to come get your daughter. Now." Her voice echoed across the room. My stomach was immediately in knots. In minutes, Tom was dressed and out the door.

There'd been issues before, meltdowns, times we needed to go talk with her and smooth things over. Now, though: A caregiver going to the hospital? Seven police officers? Nothing like this.

As I waited for Tom and Emily to return to our Encino home, I wandered from room to room, wanting to change things for her, wishing we didn't find ourselves in this situation, but unable to fix anything. Emily was our only child. A beautiful, amazing, precious young woman. She's also autistic and pretty much nonverbal. If I asked her a question, she could give me a yes or no answer, but she'd be unable to elaborate, to express verbally her pleasure or displeasure, or to open a line of dialogue with us or anyone else. This limitation made her appear, to those who failed to understand the disability, as if she were locked inside herself and incapable of making decisions or having preferences. She was unable to tell us what it was like being Emily, how the autism shaped her, or the way words, as well as the world, failed her. She couldn't tell us if she had a stomachache or a toothache or needed help in some way. She appeared to live in an isolated space to which we had repeatedly tried to gain access and failed. She was alone in there.

When her inability to communicate was coupled with frustration, the often dramatic-looking symptoms of autism—compulsive and/or repetitive behaviors, self-injury, disruptive vocalization—emerged. Simply stated, she could have meltdowns. They could happen with anyone and in any locale.

It had been a little easier when she was younger. While her outbursts, even then, were difficult, now that she was a fully grown adult and commanded space, her voice was loud and powerful, her physical presence imposing, and the incidents had grown harder to manage. Emily could act differently than other people, often in ways that could be startling.

When the call came, she was living in an apartment in Westwood with support staff and participating in a transition program at the UCLA Extension school for students with special needs. This was all part of our experiment in independent living for her, a goal encouraged and valorized by so many of our friends raising young adults with special needs. We wanted to give her the skills she'd need to live as independently as possible, preparing her for a life without Tom and me to watch over her, to speak for her, to be the buffer between Emily and the world. Since her very first diagnosis, we worried how Emily was going to manage in this world when we were gone and no longer here to be her intermediaries.

Tom and I had been older parents when Emily arrived. While most parents of young adults at our stage of the game were now looking forward to seeing their children make independent lives for themselves, we were simply hoping to get her on footing stable enough to manage without our constant intervention.

In some ways, that January call shouldn't have been quite so surprising. Over the preceding year, her meltdowns had become progressively more challenging. Recently, the agency providing her support had demanded we obtain additional behavioral services to try to rein in her conduct, and we had. We acquiesced to their request even though, after twenty-plus years of behavioral intervention, we'd found such therapies mostly ineffective with Emily. Everything we could do had already been done. As her desire for autonomy ran up against her limitations with speech, the overflow of emotions and frustrations had grown more insistent.

To have a child with autism and to be told she'll never be capable of genuine communication, that her life will always be severely limited, is to know deep and abiding grief. From our experience, a child with autism is like a person locked inside a closet at the top of a collapsed stairway, in a boarded-up house that's hidden by overgrown vines, down a driveway blocked by deadfall on a street bypassed by the highway. This closet is the entire life of the autistic individual, removed from the world. Yet the worst horror is the thought that within that closet, a single light burns brightly.

We'd seen firsthand and from a very young age the spark and animation in Emily's eyes and sensed an untold intelligence confined within her. Yet we'd been told by countless experts countless times that our dreams for her were misplaced. She'd never communicate. Her life would be forever limited. After twenty-five years we'd come to accept this reality, while still hoping it could be otherwise. On the one hand, we acknowledged the objective reality of how she presented to the world and accepted and loved her completely. We also nurtured stubborn seeds of hope that, to almost all professionals we interacted with, were irrational. Could our dream actually come to pass, that Emily might finally be able to tell us about her life? If so, she might escape some of the autism constraints that had long held her. We clung firmly to the belief that one day she might be able to free herself from the frustrations that had become so hard for her to bear.

I worried, though, that we'd been premature in thinking she was ready to live away from home. Perhaps we were deluded about what she was capable of. We had no idea how to move forward into better terrain.

What most people who witnessed her episodes didn't realize was that these behaviors were her form of communication. Without the ability to formulate words, she had no other mode of expression. We knew and understood this dynamic, yet by this point, the explosions had become an ineffective and increasingly problematic way to make herself heard. We needed to help her find another strategy.

Seven officers.

The UCLA arrangement had been a beginning, an investigation into figuring out her strengths and weaknesses. The experiment, though, was not quite working out the way we'd hoped. Despite having arranged support 24/7 to assist her in navigating the program, the campus, the community, and the social interactions, to give her the experience of living away from us, we found ourselves contacted regularly when an issue with her behavior arose.

Little things could set her off. A change of expected plans or a roadblock of any form (both literal and figurative) might result in a flare-up with distressed vocalizations, finger flapping, yelling, and other agitated behaviors that displayed her displeasure or anxiety. On more than one occasion, a meltdown in public had drawn the attention of a security guard or Trader Joe's manager who tried to intervene. While these authority figures may have had the best of intentions, their involvement sometimes escalated things and made the episode worse. In a full-scale incident, Emily might scream as if her life were being threatened. She might hit herself in the head or bite her finger. If she was trying to get someone's attention, she might get aggressive: grab, pinch, or even rake their skin with her nails. Though you'd think we'd be used to this by now, sometimes these explosions still alarmed Tom and me. When Emily was upset and made her disturbance known, even those of us who knew her kind and gentle spirit could be left reeling. I could imagine how her behavior must have been greeted by those who didn't know her or who happened to observe her in public.

Like the police, whom I kept picturing in my head gathered around her, confronting her.

I paced the house, then straightened her bedroom. I couldn't help imagining the red-and-blue police cruiser lights on her street in Westwood. Had their guns been drawn? I imagined the officers crowded around my daughter's terrified face. She would have been utterly unable to answer their questions or to explain what had happened. Her bewilderment at what unspooled must have been immense. I could protect her from only so many things in this difficult life, but not from everything. I feared that I'd failed her.

Soon, my phone was pinging. Photos of the caregiver's scratched hand and arm appeared on the screen. The raked skin and bloodied grazes along the woman's forearm looked familiar. She'd hurt me in similar ways. My head felt like it was in a vise and I was horrified by the harm she'd caused. Regardless of what triggered this reaction in Emily, aggression at this level was clearly unacceptable.

Next, I received texts from the caregiver's employer, the same woman who'd called to alert us to the incident. "The aide might need plastic surgery," she wrote. "Are you prepared to make this right?" I felt a threat had been lobbed at me by the very agency hired by the state to ensure my daughter's safekeeping. They were looking for any excuse to rid their roster of responsibility for Emily. We couldn't go on like this, no one could, most of all Emily. We needed to do something to address her behavior. But what?

AN HOUR LATER, Tom came home with Emily, who looked okay to me, not overly worked up. Pretty calm, actually. Certainly calmer than I felt.

"What happened?" I asked.

"Let's just get her to bed and then I'll fill you in," he said.

Emily went straight up to her room, unfazed by the evening's events. We both tucked her in. I smoothed her hair away from her forehead and kissed her goodnight. She turned on her side and I shut off the light.

Back in our room, Tom told me what had happened.

"It started with something about her whiteboard, where the aide writes down Emily's schedule." Emily had been upset when the aide wrote something Emily believed was wrong. Emily tried to tell her it was wrong, but the woman kept insisting it was right. Emily got agitated. She tried to get the aide to change the words on the board and that's when Emily scratched her. The aide got flustered and ran out the door, inadvertently locking herself outside and leaving Emily alone inside. The woman pounded on the door, yelling and screaming for Emily to open up. Eventually the aide called the supervisor, who sent over Cassandra, a co-owner of the service agency. She also called the police, trying to get back inside.

"It was the police who defused the situation," Tom said. "Not her caregivers. They don't know how to handle her."

Cassandra had been at the apartment when Tom arrived. The police were gone by then.

"Where's my daughter?" Tom had asked Cassandra, looking around the small apartment. "I want to take her home."

"Emily's not going to leave with you," Cassandra warned.

"What do you mean? Of course she'll go home with me."

"No, she won't. She won't do anything anyone asks her. That's the problem. She's completely obstinate."

"I'm her father. She listens to me."

"I hope you brought your toothbrush because you're going to have to spend the night. I have no other employees to put on this job, not with the way she treats the aides. She's made it clear she's not budging."

"Where is she now?" Tom asked.

"In her bedroom. She's not going to go with you. I'm telling you. She's completely uncooperative."

Tom opened the door to her bedroom. Emily looked at him from the bed where she was seated, her eyes wide.

"Emily, honey." He sat next to her. "How about this. Let's go home and see Mom. What do you say?"

With that, she stood and put on her shoes, ready to leave in an instant. When Tom walked out with Emily in tow, Cassandra was speechless. So much for Emily's recalcitrance.

Now she was finally home and we were exhausted. All that mattered was that the incident was over. As was our UCLA experiment in supported living.

Still, I couldn't sleep that night, worrying. We made it through this incident, but what about tomorrow? We needed to plot a course forward for her, establish how she'd make her way in this world when Tom and I would not be present as her mediators. There must be an answer.

We had no way to know it at the time but we were only months away from the moment our beloved daughter would finally be able to fully reveal herself to us.

1

There are different sounds I make, depending on what's going on. The first is my "thinking noise." With the thinking noise, I do a lot of high pitches and lower, almost musical sounds. It sounds like Eee-Geeee.

My next major noise is the super high-pitched squealing noise. It means I'm excited. I used to have a guttural yell for those moments, but it was too confusing and upsetting for other people, so I made a conscious change there.

That guttural yell is now my third noise. It's when I'm overwhelmed or angry, and I use it much less often nowadays.

The fourth sound is part laughter and part excited utterance. It's about looking forward to something so much that I can barely contain myself.

The fifth is the whispers and almost babbling. That shows up when I'm reaching my limit, even from good things.

I think it was my autistic brain—that part of me that helps me navigate the disorder but is not really who I am—who chose the sounds. Autistic brain is the disorder, a part of me but in some ways, not the real me.

Autistic brain is the mind space that stands between me and everything I want to do. It's the part of me that hyper focuses on sound or sight or thought and pulling away can be challenging. Autistic brain is the Emily that is a stimming storm versus the calm, quiet Emily and settled Emily that I prefer. It is distracting and makes focusing incredibly hard. It is also exhausting. Like my brain is working too hard, or perhaps too little. And my body moves and my voice does not rest and my mind is someplace else. I am still learning to move past it, sometimes a fight and sometimes I can slip out. More often, it is back and forth.

I started these noises at five or six. I don't know why these particular noises or why any noises at all. I wish autistic brain would tell me. I haven't asked before. I will.

Emily was born in October 1991. I was forty years old and had an established law practice. Like most new mothers, I could not take my eyes off my daughter, unable to get over how wonderful and perfect and beautiful she was. I didn't need to turn on the TV or talk with anyone. I could sit for hours looking at her, feeling at peace, flooded with awareness of how very lucky and blessed I was to be her mother.

She started smiling early, at only four or five weeks, offering grins to disarm even the biggest curmudgeon. She loved to look at people. My secretarial assistant was among our first visitors after her birth. As soon as she glanced at Emily, she commented, "I can't believe she's looking into my eyes. She's so attentive." Emily had a mound of curly blond hair, beautiful huge eyes, pristine skin.

People commented on Emily's charismatic presence repeatedly. We thought that's just what people said to parents of new babies, but we soon realized there was something unique about her.

Early motherhood had a few challenges I worked to overcome. Emily had arrived two weeks early, and I was unable to attend a scheduled hearing on a case in San Francisco. As I could not locate local counsel to assist, I worked to make arrangements with the court clerk and a very cooperative judge to participate in the hearing via phone from the comforts of my home. More incredibly, I pulled it off while nursing Emily in my rocking chair. It was all just so perfect.

My mother had lived a different kind of life, very much defined by her times. As a young woman, she'd worked as a bookkeeper but then stopped when she had kids. In the years when I'd been dating, she always hoped I'd marry someone wealthy and would never have to work a day in my life. My times and aspirations defined me, as much as hers did her, and I enjoyed my career and the connections I had outside of the home.

Before I met Tom, I'd been happy and mostly fulfilled as a single woman, successful in my career, and I'd even been able to invest in real estate. As a single person, I had what I needed and the financial independence to do as I wanted, whenever I chose.

My law practice was varied, which I liked as it never got boring. I had my own practice with offices first in Beverly Hills, then in Century City, and handled civil litigation matters mostly focusing on financial issues. I had perfected the 8:00 a.m. to 3:00 p.m. workday—I never ate lunch—and most afternoons could head to the Sports Connection gym on Ocean Park Avenue before going home to get ready for the evening, which often included going out. It was a perfectly fine life. Though I'd dated and had a few relationships that appeared promising, I was still hoping to meet that special someone.

Most Friday nights I showed up at my friend Wendy Moss's house, complaining about the dates I'd had that week. She was a deputy district attorney. I think her husband grew sick of me crashing their Fridays. I am more than certain it was he who encouraged her to fix me up with someone and give them back their time.

With very little warning, she did just that. She let me know I'd be contacted by one of her friends, a public defender, who she thought might be a good match. Soon, I received a call from Tom. After a few pleasantries, he asked me to dinner.

We met at an Indian restaurant for what I expected would be an hour-long meal. Over samosas, Tandoori chicken, and saag paneer, I learned that he was smart and funny with a very dry sense of humor. He playfully teased me about my corporate clients, putting himself in the Robin Hood role against my Prince John.

"If we had a dinner party and got our various clients together, we'd have just about every representation of society at the table," he said. "It would end up in a food fight." He got me to laugh at myself.

Tom remembered that night as well. "A bunch of people had been setting me up on blind dates and none of them had been any good. I was tired of it but said yes to Wendy, thinking I'd get this date over with and it wouldn't lead anywhere. Then you walked in. I was totally blown away. I wasn't expecting someone like you. Wow, you were so beautiful. From the minute we said hello, it was all so easy. Everything clicked. You were so full of life. That had never happened to me before."

When the check came, Tom didn't ask me to split the bill. He was chivalrous like that.

Though the check was closed out, we came up with reasons not to leave, another story I needed to share, a joke he needed to tell. Maybe a cup of coffee. The restaurant workers wanted to throw us out so they could go home. I looked at my watch. We'd been talking for five hours.

Driving home that night, after we'd lingered in the parking lot and reluctantly said goodbye, I completely missed my turnoff. I'd never gotten lost trying to find my own home before. Something special was happening. "That's the guy I'm going to marry," I told a close friend shortly after.

As we saw more of each other I learned to appreciate his ability to work with people—he was so much better than I was. He'd developed his cooperative qualities from having played sports as a kid, I figured. I hadn't been raised in that environment. My father was self-employed and there was no group give-and-take in my childhood. I also worked for myself and wasn't used to accommodating others, but Tom showed me how. He was very Midwestern, a quality I found comforting.

The one drawback was his taste in clothes: terrible. No-iron, poly-cotton dress shirts. A knit tie. The same ugly, light blue blazer every time. He was handsome and trim and could wear just about anything. Within a month or two of our first date, I managed to convince him to jettison the offending blazer, and then I took him shopping. After that, the clothes matched the man and he looked sharp.

Our courtship was brief. I was thirty-eight when we

married; he was forty-one. We were not committed to having children, but agreed that should we be lucky enough to get pregnant, we would be thrilled to start a family. Before I'd even met him, I'd picked out the name Emily to pay homage to my father, Manuel, who'd died five years earlier, so as to keep his memory alive. We named a favorite stuffed animal Leo the Lion, thinking, *This is for Emily.* I think we really wanted children but were afraid to admit how much.

Almost immediately after we married, Tom left the public defender's office and opened his own criminal defense practice in Beverly Hills. It goes without saying that we were doing well financially.

Then I missed my period and suddenly we were also building a family.

ONCE THE BABY came, we thought the rest of our lives would unfold the way my career had: on schedule, following a straightforward plan. Everybody else around me was birthing babies and resuming their pre-baby lives with no snags. They hired nannies and their careers continued to advance smoothly. I saw no disruption in their social lives, no curtailments of their pet projects or crimping of their travel plans. We'd be the same.

The truth is, I knew nothing about children. I'd never even babysat as a teenager; I was completely ignorant, and I'd lived on my own for so long. I was anxious a lot during the pregnancy, worrying about whether my child would be physically handicapped. I often panicked, especially at night, and was unable to sleep. In an effort to ward off the anxiety, I slept with my head at the foot of the bed, walked around the house at night, or walked outside, sharing little of my anxieties with anyone but Tom, who was more than aware of my nocturnal restlessness. I reminded myself that no one in the family had been born with any kind of disability. There may have been issues with anxiety and depression, but they were manageable and not life altering.

Of course, the early days of motherhood would not be perfect. Life, in the best circumstances, wasn't without its challenges. We'd simply follow the same trajectory everyone else had. I expected to go back to work just a few weeks after Emily was born. As a sole practitioner, I had no one in the office to pick up the slack. We hired a nanny.

Tom had similar expectations of family life. He'd watched his older brother and sister have kids, noted their joy and also seen the challenges. He was ready. "I wanted to be a great dad, to always be there for her. That was my biggest wish: to be as good a dad as I could be. Still, never in a million years did I think that we'd have a child with a disability and we'd have to deal with it."

Three weeks after her birth, I drove to work every day up and down Beverly Glen Boulevard, the winding canyon road that connects to the hills above Los Angeles where we lived. This was harder than I'd anticipated. I missed my baby daughter. I kept seeing Emmy's face in front of me as I drove. Sometimes I cried. It was so hard. I kept pumping breast milk and did what I could, continuing to nurse her until she was ten months old. Still, being away from her during the day felt like my heart was being ripped from my chest.

I comforted myself by remembering that our education, personal interests, and economic advantage assured that Tom and I would give Emily the biggest world possible. We were determined to share with her as many experiences as we could. We vowed to take her along with us on every trip, to show her this remarkable, huge life.

ALL THE SIGNS pointed toward the fact Emily was fitting into our plan just perfectly. When Emmy was about six months, we traveled to Milwaukee with her to visit Tom's family. At the airport, we rented a car, and as Tom loaded the trunk, I struggled to secure Emily's infant car seat. It was a beautiful day and Emily sat quietly as I tried to secure the car seat buckle, my exasperation building.

"Can I help you?" Tom asked, gripping the luggage, trying to assist.

"I got it," I snapped at him as my level of annoyance grew. I jiggled the connections, tightened the straps, but still couldn't figure the damn thing out.

Emily reached up from within the seat. Her eyes, always intent, had been following my every move. She was clearly aware of my irritation and decided to intervene. With her little hand, she simply and intentionally pressed down on the one button that needed to be released. That did it. Suddenly the car seat fit securely.

How did she know that? She was only six months old.

"Well, it's clear you don't need Mommy anymore, do you?" I joked, kissing her forehead.

Still, I was astounded. She understood the mechanics of the car seat better than I did.

We continued to be amazed by Emily during that trip. We drove down to Chicago looking to explore the museums and to shop on Michigan Avenue. In the Nordstrom elevator,

Emily looked up from her stroller and studied the face of each person in the confined space. So intent was her focus that I was a bit startled when the woman standing next to me said, "Wow. Your child is so engaging." Emily's stare and fixated attention were so powerful, everyone wanted to say hi to her.

It happened time and again. Later at the Tea Room at Marshall Field's we had a similar experience. Emmy kept gazing at people, boring into them. "There's a baby over there who's just staring at me," I overheard one woman tell her companion.

Months later, back in California at the pier on Manhattan Beach, the same kind of comment: "Did you see that child? The way she looked at me. Unbelievable." These instances of her concentrated visual engagement continued throughout her toddler years.

EMILY DEVELOPED LARGELY according to expected timelines, as articulated by various experts from Dr. Spock to Heidi Murkoff, author of *What to Expect When You're Expecting*. She rolled over on target at around four months, brought herself to a sitting position and stayed there by six months.

At her first birthday party, she showed us a bit more of her personality. Like all children that age, she'd been doing some scooting, crawling, and cruising on furniture. That day, though, she made up her mind that it was time to walk. She didn't toddle across the room, falling every few steps, waddling her way into our arms. She didn't allow herself to be goaded into it by the promise of applause or a reward. She simply made up her mind, stood, and walked across the room as if she'd been doing it all her life. No big deal. She was ready and simply took off.

I think of that now and connect it with the way she has approached so many things in her life. Once she makes up her mind, she goes from zero to sixty in the blink of an eye. It's just part of who she is.

Shortly after her first birthday, she was able to use single words and to call out letters and the numbers one through ten when prompted by *Sesame Street*. She fed her dolls and engaged in imaginative play. When she stood up that day and walked with such authority, it again confirmed our expectations: we were raising a special, incredible child.

HOWEVER, A FEW other incidents raised questions.

When Emmy was about four months, Tom was holding her and she grew stiff and wanted to twist out of his arms. She looked pained to be touched, to be held at all, her back rigid, her legs kicking. She screamed in anguish. Her discomfort at being embraced was clear and pointed. It scared Tom.

"I thought all babies liked to cuddle," he told me that night. "It didn't seem right."

"They're all individuals. Some like cuddling less than others," I replied. Secretly, I worried, too. I'd noticed her pulling away from me, as well. Was something amiss? *No*, I told myself. *All new parents have these thoughts. Nothing's wrong.*

While Emily could stare with razor-sharp intensity, she wasn't really making eye contact with people. There is a real difference between intently studying a person, and making actual eye contact. Emily didn't make the connection. She stared boldly, in a way that might be considered rude in an older child or adult.

There were other troubling signs. Emily hated whenever I left her for any amount of time. She became unusually traumatized when she realized I was leaving in the mornings to go to work. Yet as unhappy as she was to see me leave, she failed to greet me with joy when I came home at the end of the workday. She welcomed me home with a tantrum. Not really knowing whether she wanted me home or gone, I was left to guess and elected to shorten my workdays to spend more time with her. That improved things marginally. Still, whenever she heard the word "bye," even when I was hanging up on a phone call, she became very upset. I kept wondering if something was wrong.

2

I knew I was not living up to their expectations for me. They expected me to speak. My frustration was huge. But not because I badly wanted to speak. At that time, I was just as happy to stay silent. I just felt sad that I wasn't able to do what they wanted me to.

Being young was at times a very confusing experience. Sometimes it felt like there were words and language spinning around me constantly. When I was very young I had difficulty focusing on anything that was not whatever my mind was currently hyperaware of.

I spent a lot of time with my parents. I have always felt safest with them. They protected me fiercely. Even today, their smell brings me comfort as it did as a toddler. And not like a perfume smell, just themselves.

When I was very little they always zipped around me. Like Dad has always taken the stairs two at a time. They have never been idle people. They were always busy with me in terms of going outside to play and going out to the park but also just as themselves. The things I remember most strongly are their faces. *I remember they looked at me so often like they were memorizing every detail of me. Their faces have changed so little, I feel. In fact in general they have changed so little but they were far busier then. My mom would talk so fast. I knew even very young the calming balance Dad had.*

I have lived in the same house forever so I still imagine them here zipping all over the house. I remember them often dressed nicely and Mom clicking around in her heels. I loved that sound. We have always had dinner together, have always sat together to eat. The smells of dinner, even when I was very small, were comforting. I have always loved sweets. I loved ice cream. I loved Sesame Street. I loved my home, it was and still is my safe place.

I think that my parents wanted me to have the opportunity to try everything. They taught me how to ride a bike and how to roller skate. I saw other children doing those things, so of course I felt good doing them. My parents are and were great teachers. They always talked to me normally. They constantly chatted with me, even if I couldn't chat back. I believe that was very beneficial to me.

They always celebrated me. Anything I learned was celebrated. Birthdays were always celebrated. For parties my mom always loved to dress me up. Mom was very stylish herself.

When I was very little, I was mostly very happy. The thing that confused me most was language. It's like I could not process words. I could not hold or direct my focus. It took longer for me to learn things because I could not break out of that unfocused, autistic brain.

"Does your child have some hearing difficulty?" the woman teaching the music class asked me, trying to be polite. "Is it possible she's deaf?"

I was stunned. I hadn't noticed anything amiss with her hearing. At home, she'd recognize the *Barney* theme song on the TV from three rooms away and come running.

Like many new parents, we'd read that early exposure to music advances a child's intellectual growth, so we'd signed her up for this class run by a professional violinist and her sister, also a musician. The sisters played different instruments for the kids, including drums and percussion instruments. The other children bopped their heads, or stood and swayed, or clapped their hands, interacting with the sounds. Emily didn't react or respond to the music at all.

What I should have noticed was how completely nonresponsive she was in that class, even when the cymbals were clanging and the drums pounding. The cacophony never bothered her in the least, which is probably why the teacher raised the issue. To this day, I don't understand why Emily, who is hypersensitive to so many sounds, could sit with those harsh noises. I have been next to her in a car with the top down when a gang of motorcyclists roars past and she never flinches. If Tom coughs or sneezes, however, she reacts viscerally. There was something sensitive and different about her hearing.

We decided to have her tested. A brain-stem assessment concluded that her senses were fully functional. Emily was not deaf.

Other indicators that Emily might not be progressing developmentally emerged after her first birthday. Emily and I attended a Mommy and Me class hosted by a psychologist where I noticed the other kids cuddling with their mothers, wanting closeness, snuggling on their laps. Emily was more independent, and actually, I was proud of her for it. The other children refused to leave their mothers' space, tentative and a bit scared of the world. Not Emily. She was up and about, checking out the room, exploring, examining things. *Look at the way she just does what she wants. She's a strong girl who knows her own mind.* I was pleased by what I viewed as her independence.

THE CONTRADICTIONS CONTINUED to pile up. Tom took Emily to a Daddy and Me–type class at the Encino Community Center. The fathers and children were all gathered around colorful wooden blocks for building towers. Tom sat next to a man with his young son. The boy quickly built a tower, balancing the blue, yellow, and red blocks, one on top of the other, taking obvious joy in constructing the ever-changing configuration, laughing and smiling as he did so, pleasing his father.

"Look, Em." Tom held out a block. "You can put it like this." He mimed the action.

She didn't care, didn't want to hear what he was saying.

Tom showed her how to start building a tower. "You place the block like this."

Emily didn't respond.

"Come on, Emily. Don't you want to build a tower?" His voice became pleading.

No matter what he did, he couldn't get her engaged. She refused to look at the blocks, wouldn't touch them. She was almost scared of them.

"I was dying inside," Tom said. "Just begging her to put something together. God, it was so hard to watch this other kid. I don't know if it was shame or embarrassment, but when no one was looking, I quickly built a tower so I could pretend Emily had done it like the others."

Meanwhile, Emily was way behind in expressing herself with language, though she could count when prompted and could follow along saying letter names. She also screamed a lot.

Amid those concerns, there were little glimpses of hope. Tom was at the mailbox one day when Emily was leaving with the nanny for an outing. "I go play," she said to him. A full sentence. Of her own initiation. We were thrilled. Again, we applauded what we saw as her autonomy, her progress, the meeting of a developmental milestone. She hadn't engaged with the tentative stumbling that most other children do when they learn to speak. She hadn't offered a sentence composed of half-formed words. She articulated one complete, declarative sentence. Surely this was the beginning of her late-bloomer approach to language. We waited.

AFTER THE DADDY and Me episode, Tom was troubled. He began researching, which led him to the *Diagnostic and Statistical Manual of Mental Disorders* (DSM)* in his law office, one of his reference books for all of the work his firm did in the mental health field. He raised questions at dinner.

"Don't you notice how she's not making eye contact?" he asked.

"She's just easily distracted."

---

* The DSM was initially drafted in 1952. It has gone through several revisions and is currently known as the DSM-5. Due to modifications in the DSM in the years since Emily was diagnosed, when reference is made in this text to the DSM, please always consider the year of the reference.

"I know. Maybe it's something else."

"What are you talking about?" I challenged him. "She's fine."

"People say that lack of eye contact is a symptom of certain conditions."

"What conditions?" I was getting mad. "What are you suggesting?"

"Well, some books talk about autism." Tom knew the word was toxic.

"Isn't that a bit of a reach?"

"What about the toe-walking? A lot of experts say that's a pretty clear indicator."

I was in denial of it all, but one thing I couldn't deny was the fact that Emily had started walking on her toes shortly after she started walking. The professionals speculated— almost all of the endless parade that would soon become part of our life—that autistic children may prefer to walk on their tiptoes because doing so provides sensory stimulation not present when one walks on the entire foot. At the time, toe-walking was widely recognized as a sure sign of autism.

"She doesn't do it all the time," I countered. "It's only occasionally."

"And the screaming?"

"She was always a colicky baby. When we lived on Mulholland Drive, remember how we had to walk back and forth with her at night so she could look at the lights of the city until she calmed? Maybe it's just extended colic?"

On some level, though, it was getting increasingly impossible to deny the signs. I didn't want to see what was right in front of me.

I tried to convince myself that Tom was leaping to

conclusions. We had evidence she was brilliant. There was the car seat incident. And the first-birthday walking. These phrases became mantras I repeated to myself to forestall the other data: She wasn't babbling like a lot of other children her age. Not saying "mama" or "dada." Nor was she pointing, which is a well-known preverbal act.

Tom, meanwhile, spent time in the Beverly Hills library near his office, checking out books and reading up on autism. "In the back of my mind, I knew what it was," Tom told me later. "I was very upset, but I didn't want to show it. I thought, *All right, we have this coming. I know what's happening. We'll just have to deal with it. I will give a thousand percent.*"

Still, I was convinced Emily was bright and exceptional. I held on to that regardless of what Tom thought.

When Emily was about fourteen months, as if to speak aloud my desires for her, I told Tom, "I can't wait to hear Emily talk. I know she has so much to say." Her words would come any day now. We'd been thinking about having a second child, and I'd decided that the timing would be right when Emily started talking. I kept waiting.

WE ATTENDED A birthday party for one of the children in our Mommy and Me group when Emily was about sixteen months. The family had constructed a small maze made of plastic blocks in their yard. It was a pretty simple exercise and all the parents were cheering and clapping for the kids as they entered and plotted their way through the maze. We tried to lure Emily into participating, but she wouldn't get anywhere near the maze. Either she knew she couldn't do it, or she was in some way afraid of it. Whatever the reason, her refusal scared me. She was not complying with the norms of childhood and I didn't like it.

Was it possible Tom was right? The woman who ran the Mommy and Me class was a psychologist. She would know about developmental delays and other childhood issues. Privately, away from the other parents, I asked her, "Emily is fine, isn't she? Developmentally, I mean."

"Oh, you have nothing to worry about," she reassured me. "She is so independent. She'll be the president of the United States one day." Yes, she was independent. She did not cuddle with me the way the other kids did. I wasn't sure if independence at sixteen months was a good thing.

I tried to believe the expert, but day by day, my instincts aligned with what Tom had been saying. Something was wrong.

THE TURNING POINT came on a trip to Florida to attend a bar mitzvah for Tom's nephew. Emily was eighteen months old and I was sure at any moment we were about to hear her utter her first full sentences.

The trip started off fine. On the way to the hotel, in fact, we passed a Burger King. From the back seat of the car we heard Emily say the letter "B" a few times in succession. She'd seen the "B" in the neon sign. Not only was she saying the letter, but she was demonstrating letter recognition, an indication she'd be reading and speaking before we knew it.

We attended the reception following the ceremony and Emily was adorable in a flowered dress, complete with little Mary Jane shoes and tights. When the band started playing nineties pop music in the ballroom, Emily toddled to the center of the empty dance floor and started to wiggle her little butt, her diaper peeking out from under her dress. The entire party of a hundred and fifty guests stopped to watch her moves. *Of course nothing is wrong*, I admonished myself. *Look, she's got such a dynamic personality, she can keep a hundred and fifty people enthralled.*

That night, we left her with a teenage friend of the family in our hotel room while Tom and I returned to the celebration. Once we left the room, though, Emily became very agitated. The babysitter didn't know what to do and decided to tough it out. By the time we returned a few hours later, Emily's face was swollen from crying, snot all over her cheeks, her eyes red and her voice raw. She'd been standing in her crib the whole time we'd been gone, just screaming.

"I couldn't get her to stop," the babysitter said.

I know it sounds crazy or superstitious, but looking back, she was not the same after that. Before that night, she'd been able to understand things that were spoken to her, to raise her hands to have her dress changed, to come when called. Occasionally, she'd even said a word or two. We'd seen her engage in imaginative play, and though she didn't care much about toys, ones that had become familiar to her she'd occasionally play with or hold.

For whatever reason, from that night on, the progress toward language that Emily had been making—saying "I go play" that one time, recognizing and pronouncing the letter "B" from the fast-food sign—simply evaporated. We were moving backward.

3

I kept wondering, as she pulled further away from us and inside herself, where did the person I knew from birth to eighteen months of age go? She was in there and that person was impressive, but where was she now? The thought haunted me for all the coming years when she didn't make the progress I'd hoped for; when she became more remote and ever harder to reach. I couldn't let go of the child I knew. The precociousness, the liveliness, the initial engagement. I couldn't accept—never *did* accept—that the person who started off in my body and whom I'd seen smile with the impact of a thousand-watt bulb, was no longer there but hidden now in some impenetrable shell.

FOR EMILY'S SECOND birthday I planned a party. I decorated the house and ordered a special cake. A clown with a crazy wig and costume came to entertain the kids, mostly children of family friends. They all lined up to have their faces painted and ran around the yard, playing games with each other. Not Emily. Rather than engage with the other children, she played on the swings by herself, content in her own company.

"Go play with the others," I encouraged. She wouldn't.

She barely tolerated us singing "Happy Birthday" and blowing out the candles. As the party unfolded, she decided she'd had enough. She left the festivities and marched through the family room and to her bedroom to be alone, leaving us all in the backyard.

I felt like my legs had been cut out from underneath me. I watched her go, my heart in my throat. I noted her complete lack of interest in the social activities of the day, no interest in the birthday presents or the children or the games.

We have a picture from that day of Tom holding her, this beautiful child in a burgundy flowered dress with a crocheted collar. Her eyes are vacant and sad. Deeply sad. To this day, neither Tom nor I can bear looking at that photo. It was as if she'd lost her light.

A FEW DAYS later we took Emily to her pediatrician for her annual checkup. After the examination, we expressed our suspicions with the kindly, older doctor, listing the warning signs we'd documented.

The doctor nodded. "My colleague across the hall is a specialist in developmental-behavioral pediatrics at Children's Hospital Los Angeles. Let me call over there. Maybe she can work you in today. She only comes into this satellite office once a week."

The specialist was able to see us right away. We met her in an examination room that was small and windowless, painted a pale bluish-gray, with two chairs for the parents and a child-size plastic table with a chair. The only relief from the sterile blandness was a collection of generic toys intended, I suppose, for the examining doctor to use to engage the child.

The specialist, who appeared to be in her forties, entered the room. She didn't talk to Emily, didn't use any of those toys, just clinically evaluated her for a brief moment. I couldn't understand how she could make a credible diagnosis without any effort to engage our daughter. Now, twenty-five years later with the wisdom of hindsight, I understand how recognizable the disability is.

She turned her attention fully to us. "What's your worst fear?"

"Autism." I said the word aloud, the word we'd once whispered in bed to each other, that we'd researched and parsed and tried to dismiss. The word that kept showing up again and again, no matter how many rationalizations I came up with; the word that cast a dark cloud over our lives. I hated that damn word. And now, I'd said it aloud to an expert in the field. I waited for her to dismiss the naivete of a new parent.

"Well, you're right to be worried."

I held my breath.

The doctor explained that, in her opinion, Emily had pervasive developmental disorder (PDD).

She didn't say *autism*! My shoulders dropped about four inches. I looked at Tom, raising my eyebrow. All those concerns were for naught! I took his hand. Emily was okay.

The doctor must have seen the relief on my face because she quickly shook her head, clarifying what she meant. "This is the diagnosis given to children before they're school-age."

"I don't understand."

"Sometimes children are slow developers and have not

yet emerged with all the characteristics required for an official autism diagnosis, so the preferred practice is to give it time."

"You mean . . . ?" Tom asked.

"As she ages, I'm pretty certain she will be recategorized as autistic. In either event, whether autism or PDD, the interventions and therapies are the same."

"You're telling me that she basically has autism but it's too early to call it that?" I asked. That brief moment of hope made this diagnosis all the more devastating.

"Yes," the doctor said. "Your child is autistic."

The doctor sat there, completely without emotion. Her words fell on us like sledgehammers. How I wish we'd been with someone with a better bedside manner, who could have understood our suffering in that moment, who could have delivered the news with a little empathy or kindness. I felt unmoored. Our daughter just stared at us, oblivious to what was unfolding. Young children are generally aware of their surroundings and would certainly note the distress of their parents, and Emily typically did. At that moment, though, Emily was unconcerned. I didn't want to get hysterical with her in the room, but panic was growing inside me. I started to cry. Tom put his arm around me.

As if reading off a checklist, the doctor recited places we could go next for intervention. She was so damn officious.

This couldn't be happening. The little voice of denial in my head kept rallying. I wanted to show this doctor that she was wrong. *Watch us*, I wanted to say, *we'll do whatever it takes. We'll find the top specialists, explore all the treatments, and then she'll be fine. By the time she starts school we'll have the autism under control. We are smart people.*

We have the means. We'll hire experts. We won't stop until we've straightened this out. Whatever it takes, we'll do it. Watch us!

I crumbled a little bit as we left the office, the sun stinging my eyes. On the five-minute drive home, I kept looking back at the car seat to see Emily, her huge eyes taking it all in. Our beautiful child. I had no idea of the journey we were about to set out on, the implications of the diagnosis and where it would all lead. Still, I was ready to fight for her with all I had.

DESPITE THE CONCLUSION reached by that specialist, we were unwilling to wholeheartedly accept the diagnosis. We'd both been schooled in the idea that you always need a second opinion; until we had a hard-and-fast, undeniable determination established by at least two medical professionals, I was not ready to acknowledge this reality and fully take it in.

Tom, meanwhile, continued his research as more symptoms emerged. Emily demonstrated no back-and-forth communication via smiles and facial expressions, no babbling, no pointing to objects to ask for them. Tom tried to work on getting her to play with toys—to get her to even just touch one could be a challenge. Once he tried with a red toy truck, a little matchbox truck from a set her grandmother had sent. He showed her how it worked and how, if you pulled it along the ground, its wheels would spin. When he tried to get her to touch it, she screamed and jerked away from him and the car as if he were burning her. She was terrified of it.

Still, we held on to our hopes that Emily was, as my mother suggested, just a "late talker." After all, Emily was so animated, always smiling at people: she must be okay. Emily continued walking on her toes, however.

"Flat feet, Emily, flat feet," we said.

She did as instructed.

Inevitably, though, the toe-walking returned.

I have a mind that soaks up all that is around me. I have an interesting relationship with words and languages, regarding the ease with which I write. I can see a picture or hear a song and experience it many different ways each time. I hold information in a way that I can sometimes see it before me. My senses allow me to experience things on a greater level than most, I think. The same way, I experience great emotion, even if it takes time to process them.

Things got frustrating, especially when autism stuff was occurring with me. I knew I wasn't fully in control and I didn't like that. I was aware I was different, of course. I overheard conversations—I can hear everything in this damn house. I remember my parents' blank faces, I could see the disconnect they felt. There's just so much unmapped emotion from that time.

It's a strange thing to have to realize that you are not like everyone else. It was sometimes frustrating knowing that I had my way of doing things that was not efficient or typical. With that being said, I would not change who I am now . . . much.

4

The video was of a girl with autism, trying to comb her hair. The child, about twelve, held the comb to the side of her head and looked at the camera with a blank face and empty eyes. She appeared to be fully catatonic as she pulled the comb down the side of her face, not catching a single strand of hair. She didn't notice.

The video playing on the VCR shook me to my core. To this day, I still see images of that little girl in my mind. It was a mockery of a child grooming herself.

"You're telling me, this is what I can expect for my daughter?" I spoke to the screen before punching the button to turn the video off and tossing the remote onto the coffee table. I couldn't accept this possibility. Wouldn't accept it.

MARIAN SIGMAN WAS the name that kept coming up in the days following our meeting with the doctor from Children's Hospital. Dr. Sigman was a developmental and clinical psychologist who cofounded the UCLA Center for Autism Research and Treatment (CART). Her work focused on the biological and environmental factors that contribute to social and communicative deficits in autism. The fact that her office was nearby at UCLA was a boon, though, to be honest, I would have gone to Timbuktu.

As Dr. Sigman was very much in demand, we were unable to get an appointment immediately so in the meantime, we read everything we could get our hands on to understand what was happening, what our options were, how best to advocate and understand what to do for Emily. We were certain that with our prompt intervention and strong will, we'd wrestle whatever the issue was to the ground, make it give up its secrets. By the time she was school-age, this would all be behind us.

I asked Tom if he would take Emily to the appointment with Dr. Sigman without me. I was leaning on him, upset at the whole idea of Emily being autistic. The diagnosis had shaken me deeply and now I was downright terrified that the opinion might be confirmed. I didn't want to hear it. If I refused to go and listen to what this new doctor had to say, I could keep it from being real. Magical thinking, I know, but I held on to whatever flimsy reed I could find. Rather than make space for such an unacceptable reality in my life, I buried myself in my work. While my job was challenging, everything in my field was based on rules and laws, things that made sense to me in ways that life increasingly didn't. I wanted to control those elements I still could.

As a mother, every part of me fought against applying the label *autistic* to Emily. Even later, when she was in elementary school and it was obvious she was on the spectrum, when a parent asked me if Emily was autistic, I said no. I didn't want her to be pigeonholed. Though I soon became more willing to accept the diagnosis—really, I had no choice—I long remained unwilling to share the diagnosis with others. Keep in mind, this was a quarter of a century ago. Perceptions of what it means to be autistic have changed radically in that time. As an analogy to understand the stigma we were fighting, consider that back then, it was also discreditable to have seen a psychiatrist. Workers went out of their way to keep their employer from knowing about their mental health history, going so far as to pay cash rather than use their health insurance benefits lest they become tarred by that shameful brush. To be upfront about such challenges was to commit a kind of career suicide. The same was true for autism. No one talked about it or knew what to expect. A heap of shame came with the label—not shame for me, as the parent, but rather, indignity and dishonor for Emily. Her future would be truncated by the diagnosis; people would make limiting judgments about her, based not on facts or observations, but purely on the title that got hung around her neck. I didn't want that life for her.

She was capable of so much, even if I couldn't prove it to others. Besides, until we knew for sure what was going on, until we had proof that she was not capable of leading a neurotypical life, I refused to allow other people's categorizations of my daughter to limit her. I didn't want her to be left out of the larger world, whatever her limitations might be. Somehow, I knew she *could* be in the world, *would* be part of the world. I wanted that for her with every fiber of my being.

My determination was bred in the bone. I've always been stubborn. When I was a toddler, according to my mother, I said "I do it self" to almost every situation I faced. I wanted to be independent and self-supporting from the get-go. That characteristic really flourished in caring for Emily.

Part of my determination stems from being the second child, and female to boot, in our Jewish family. I joke that my parents dropped me off at kindergarten and then picked me up at the end of high school, and that's basically true. I was completely overshadowed by my older brother's brilliance. He was the only boy and the eldest; everyone bowed down to him. I used to overhear my father talk to him in his study, making sure he did well in school, overseeing his young life. I was excluded from those kinds of talks; my parents had zero expectations of me.

"What will happen with Valerie?" my mother asked my father one time, unaware that I could hear.

"She'll just marry well and that will be that."

This attitude infuriated me and fired me up to prove them wrong. I'd show them what I was capable of. I can't say that my determination in life was anything but bred in the bone, but their attitudes toward me may have strengthened my resolve.

WHEN TOM CAME home after the appointment, my heart broke at the sight of him. He could barely look me in the face and his shoulders were slumped.

He shook his head. "Dr. Sigman agreed," he said. "She's autistic. I have a list of people we can contact to get help for her. Behaviorists, speech therapists. I just . . ." His voice cracked. "It's so hard."

For all his devastation at the diagnosis, Tom had been impressed by the doctor and trusted her. "She told me about what we could expect. None of it was positive." Still, unlike me, he didn't and wouldn't give in to horrible fear or anxiety. "This is the situation we're dealing with. What can we do immediately to make it better?"

AT THANKSGIVING A week or so later we told only the people closest to us, including Tom's mother, brother, and sister. Earlier, when I'd told my mother, she'd refused to believe it. There were no offers from any of the family members to assist us in any way—and there never would be. They were certainly all very sorry to hear this news, but that was about it. It was the start of a very lonely battle.

Even worse, some in the family actually blamed me and Tom, claiming our "parenting style" (whatever that was supposed to mean) was the cause of the disability. That hurt deeply. We were all alone.

DR. SIGMAN HAD told Tom about a young woman doing significant work with autistic children. "See if you can get in to see her," the doctor had suggested.

Doreen Granpeesheh is now known for the Center for Autism and Related Disorders (CARD), the organization she founded in the early nineties to provide behavioral intervention to individuals with autism and related disorders. She is now well recognized as a leader in the field, having been trained as a psychologist and behavior analyst at UCLA. She had been a protégé of Ivar Lovaas, a professor at UCLA famous for his early intervention techniques for children with autism.

Lovaas developed a methodology called discrete trial training (DTT) as an intervention technique. It is a structured, instructional procedure, much like tutoring, that breaks down tasks into simple subunits to shape skills. The technique uses prompts, modeling, and positive reinforcement to facilitate learning. Doreen had served as Lovaas's senior clinical supervisor and had worked with the families involved in his groundbreaking 1987 study documenting the progress of nine out of nineteen children who, through the use of intensive behavioral intervention including DTT, had acquired sufficient academic and language skills to be placed in a regular classroom.

We spoke to Doreen and learned that unlike Lovaas, she did not use aversives in her protocol, but had developed an adapted version of DTT and was also employing applied behavior analysis (ABA) to change and modify the more interfering behaviors demonstrated by her clients. In no time, we had a plan in place. Emily, just two years old, would participate in twenty hours a week of one-on-one discrete trials and other services with the behavioral providers in our home, under Doreen's supervision, as well as weekly family appointments with the entire "team"—Doreen, the behaviorists, and us.

"EMILY, THIS IS Tricia. She is a friend of Mommy's." I introduced the first behaviorist who came to our door, a ballerina who supported herself working for CARD. All the women who came to work with Emily were young, mostly in their twenties. As best as I can recall, all had undergraduate degrees, and some were pursuing advanced degrees in psychology. Back then, I do not believe special training and certification to provide home-based services were mandated; I don't know if they had any formal training beyond whatever Doreen had taught them.

We made space for Tricia and the rotating group of behaviorists in the spare bedroom upstairs. They'd take Emily in that room and shut the door. We were welcome to come watch, of course, but didn't want to be a distraction. Plus, it was simply too painful to observe.

Five to six hours a day, four days a week, Tricia or a behaviorist sat with Emily, asking her to do specific tasks. *Look at me. Hand me the toy. Touch your nose.* Over and over and over again, the same commands, the nonstop orders to perform. Tricia and her ilk meticulously documented Emily's progress on these seemingly benign tasks that were part of DTT.

The young women all spoke in childish voices, full of energy and exaggeration. "Good job!" they said again and again in such a high-pitched tone that it made me want to cover my own ears. It must have been so frightening and intense for Emily. Their tone of voice and hyperbolic praise were insulting, at least to me, as if they didn't understand how bright my little girl really was.

Over and over, they noted how many times they made a request before Emily did what was asked. They offered her miniature M&M's or tiny pieces of cookie as rewards. Goals were set each week for reducing the number of requests needed to elicit the specified action. The food was meant as a reinforcer, not a reward, but that distinction for a two-year-old wasn't really clear.

I pleaded with them to stop the rewards, particularly the food. Verbal praise was okay, but the fact that she could accomplish what they wanted should be a reward in and of itself. I was ignored.

With the invasion of this army of behaviorists, our lives were reordered. It was the beginning of the regimentation of our way of life, an endless race from therapist to therapist, as our days were filled with attending to Emily's needs, as defined by her disability. I was convinced that, if we gave 100 percent to these recommended therapies, by the time Emily entered kindergarten, this autism puzzle would be solved. Again, magical thinking.

Based on what we'd been told by the experts, this behavioral intervention was our best shot at giving Emily a semblance of a normal life. In some ways, it felt like electroshock therapy, as dramatic and even as violent, the way it shook up our days, like an earthquake displacing everything we knew, how we interacted, the very foundation of our lives. Still, we had to get Emily to return to us, to interrupt the way she was withdrawing from the world. We had to act soon to get her back before she disappeared entirely.

Emily hated every moment of the therapy. She didn't want to do what was being asked. She cried when the behaviorists arrived at our front door and in no time, her screams and shrieking filled our home, sending me and Tom into hiding, trying to blot out her wailing and bawling. She fought back and resisted, wanting nothing to do with the therapy. The behaviorists, meanwhile, just noted the data: what percentage of requests were met with success, how many times she had to be asked to touch her nose before she actually did so. And so on, ad nauseum.

"HOW CAN EMILY be benefiting if she's screaming all the time?" my mother asked during one of her visits.

We refused to acknowledge that truth, as the alternative was to do nothing and that was simply not an option.

"This is what we were told we have to do," we responded. "By the experts." It was the only answer we had.

We hunkered down as if in crisis mode, willing to do anything necessary, even subject our child to activities that clearly made her miserable, hoping it would bring her back to us.

Weekly, we met with Doreen in Encino to review the progress. We hated the constant collecting of data on Emily. The clinical ways the behaviorists worked with her made me feel as if Emily weren't a beautiful child, our precious daughter, but a horse to be broken.

AFTER MONTHS OF therapy, Emily followed simple commands. She still screamed regularly, but the behaviors began to shift. She listened to us a little more intently, making eye contact occasionally, even following a bit of what we said. Even the toe-walking disappeared at some point.

Slowly, Emily gained the ability to execute certain tasks. The progress was laudable, and I prayed it would put her back on the road to a more normal life. There was hope.

We changed everything about our lives to accommodate Emily's therapies. One of us always had to be present when services were delivered in our home, so Tom moved his law practice from Beverly Hills into the house to be with Emily as often as possible. I moved my practice from Century City to nearby Tarzana so we could each take turns with her. If I had a day in court, Tom stayed home to be with Emily. If it was his turn to be in court, I stayed home. The cost of the behavior intervention, meanwhile, was staggering. To finance the behavioral therapy, we decided to sell the investment property I'd bought years earlier when I was single.

"I bought it as a hedge against a rainy day," I told Tom. "*This* is our rainy day. If we don't get our arms around this situation, she won't have a future."

What frustrated me the most was to learn that my ways of doing things would be expected to change. They wanted me to sit like this, be more quiet, look this way when someone speaks. Having that control was just not available to me at that young of an age. I have always liked to please people and I truly put forth effort.

I sometimes wonder why behavior therapy doesn't have more broken-down categories to accommodate the differences of people, and why it lacks the understanding that people like me have a disconnect between what's being asked and what I was capable of doing.

I hate saying it, but so many things they asked, I could not do—not because I didn't understand or not want to learn. There was a lot of information coming in yet it was as if my body just couldn't make sense of the information and process it to then do what was asked.

I did a lot of screaming at that time. I yelled. Screaming is something I have worked very hard on to get to where I am now, where I have some control over it. Before, I had no tools, and once the frustration and confusion piled on, I became overloaded and I would scream. I couldn't stop myself once I got going.

Also, having the behaviorists come into my home always made me weary. I wasn't able to get away. That feeling of frustration and dislike of my space being invaded lingered over me when anyone was here.

For me, autism put an interesting layer into the idea of motivation, especially considering that reward or compensation of some form is a common tool used in behavior modification. The tiny piece of candy offered as a reward for raising my left hand may have left a bitter appeal in my mind to the idea of extrinsic motivation. It really just boils down to this: behavior modification wasn't a particularly effective motive for me.

As a student now, a very different one, there is some understanding. I wouldn't be able to sit in a college classroom today without some of those things they were so adamant on teaching me, but I believe that it boils down to the lack of motivation when I was younger. I had nothing at the time that made it worth all the rules.

5

A handful of children and their parents were already in the play yard when we arrived at the Magic Years Nursery School, the most sought-after preschool in our community. It was Emily's preschool admissions interview; she was three. I wanted her to attend a typical preschool like all the other children we knew; I wanted as typical a life for her as possible.

Everyone in our Encino neighborhood raved about this school. I'd even heard of neighbors who'd enrolled their children while still in utero. It was that kind of place, supercompetitive.

"You better get her on the list right away because it's going to be really hard to get her in there," one friend said.

When we arrived for the group interview, the head of the school greeted us. I hadn't told her about Emily's diagnosis and I didn't now. I wanted her to see Emily for who she was, not based on a label applied to her. I was nervous.

I observed how the woman watched each child in the group, making mental notes, deciding who would get the golden ticket providing entrance to this world of privilege, and who would be left out. All the parents appeared anxious, hoping their kids would sufficiently impress this woman.

As the parents fretted, kids dug at the sand table with shovels and buckets while others splashed at the water table and pushed toy boats. Still others played house or dress-up with the toys provided. Thankfully, there was also a swing set. Emily always loved swinging.*

If Emily's ability to swing could get her into the school, she'd be home free.

"I need to see her interact with the other children," the woman said. "I'd like to see her capacity for imaginative play."

"Emmy, honey, how about if you go and play with the other kids?"

Reluctantly, she left the swing, but rather than join the other children, she stood there, unsure of what to do. Kids ran about her, pretended to be wild animals and spacemen, splashed water and shrieked with joy. Anyone can look at a playground and see how the kids engage with each other. If one of the children isn't engaging, she stands out.

Emily stood out.

The director of the school declined to accept her into the

---

* We are taught that we have five senses to give us information about the world: sight, hearing, touch, taste, and smell. However, there are actually *two* additional senses: the vestibular system (focused in the inner ear, giving us information about our head position and how/if we're moving in space) and the proprioceptive system (giving us information about our body's position in the world: which way we're facing, how close we are to other objects, et cetera). Since many of those with neurological disabilities, including those with autism, have underdeveloped vestibular and proprioceptive systems, swinging and rocking are activities they gravitate toward. These behaviors calm them because they stimulate these systems and assist in providing the information that helps the person to integrate that data with their other five senses.

program. In turning Emily down, though, she gave me deep insight into my daughter.

"Emily doesn't know what's expected of her," the woman told me.

Over the years, I've come to see the great wisdom of that statement. This perspective frames everything about Emily, even now. She doesn't do what people expect of her; she doesn't meet the rubric. This is an important part of her autism. She's marching to a different drummer. There's a lot of good in that. Sometimes she does *differently*, often something to be celebrated, though it's not often what's expected.

She needed a road map, to be told: "Emily, come here. Let me show you what to do." I think that would have been a better test of her competency for preschool, because once she's shown what to do, she's a champ.

AFTER THE MAGIC Years, Tom and I sought out other preschools. The interview process was similar at all schools and categorically humiliating.

"Will you take our beautiful daughter into your school? We'll pay the outrageous tuition you charge. We'll pay for a full-time aide to help her. We'll donate. We'll do whatever you say."

The answers were universally disheartening.

"We're not the place for you."

"We're not well equipped to meet your daughter's needs."

"We believe she'd be better served elsewhere."

The excuse of not being well equipped always irritated me. You don't need to be well equipped, only willing. No preschools were, until we found a low-key Montessori school in

Tarzana run by two women. The families there were more cooperative than competitive. It was a good fit. With the assistance of a one-on-one aide, Alison Appleby, a UCLA student who would go on to become a well-respected educational therapist, the experience was a success. With the support provided to her, Emily was able to navigate and participate in the preschool experience, and was not isolated from her peers.

A FRIEND OF mine from college, Kathy Anderson, came to visit us from Bishop where she worked as an English teacher. Together, the three of us went to Genesta Park in Encino. Kathy took Emily on her own and I watched as they interacted with each other. Something was different. Kathy spoke to Emily as if she were an equal. Emily paid rapt attention to every word Kathy spoke. She was engaged in a way I hadn't seen before. The light went on in my head. We needed to keep her engaged, to surround her with smart people who would challenge her and ask her to come up to their level. From that day forth, we only hired caregivers who were well educated and would model this behavior with Emily.

AS EMILY NEARED kindergarten age, I visited countless schools to examine the opportunities. I still didn't know which path to choose. I wanted her in a regular classroom if possible. Meanwhile, the hours upon hours of therapy with Doreen's behavioral team frustrated me. The pace of change, which had always been glacial, had slowed to a halt. Yes, there was a little progress—she could look at us and point to the color green; she was able to resist walking on her toes most of the time. No matter what those data sheets might demonstrate, though, it was obvious to me that behavioral therapy was no longer having the intended effect. As far as I was concerned, she had made no progress with speech and her social interactions remained extremely challenged.

I looked around for additional modalities. I briefly tried speech therapy, only to find the therapist more concerned about me—"You need to learn to take better care of yourself, Valerie"—than helping Emily communicate. Of course I was a wreck. The number of hours I spent working with the behaviorists, finding preschools for Emily, dealing with her tantrums, looking into formal school options, on top of my full-time legal practice, had worn me out.

My quest for school options took me all over the county of Los Angeles. I heard of a school in Pasadena, Villa Esperanza, some thirty miles from our home, that was being raved about. Even though it was so far away, if it worked for Emily, I was all in. I was very surprised to find on the day of the tour that there were many parents in attendance from the Encino area. Everyone was looking for the perfect fit!

Speech pathologist Alicia Elliott, in her fifties with short dark hair, radiated such caring and kindness, it almost knocked me back when I first met her at Villa Esperanza. She was soft-spoken, very warm. After years of the behaviorist's dispassion, this feeling of kindheartedness and palpable concern was magnetic. The minute Alicia started talking about her work with autistic children, I was hooked. Not only was she enthusiastic and sincere, she'd had success with so many types of kids. I felt how much she cared by the way she described her clients. She inspired me.

While the school she worked at had its appeal, I quickly saw it wasn't a good option for Emily, particularly given the distance we'd have to travel. Still, Alicia's presence and expertise stuck with me. I took her card and slipped it into my purse, thinking that one day I would need it.

EMILY'S TENURE AT the Montessori preschool, meanwhile, was coming to an end. A few days before graduation, the two women who ran the program pulled Tom and me aside.

"We don't think it's a good idea for you to bring Emily to graduation. With her noises, her yelling, you know, it might disrupt the day for the rest of the kids."

"But—" we protested.

"Please don't bring her."

I was furious. Emily had finally found her place at a school and had felt welcomed. She'd worked to graduate like the others. She was a part of the class and deserved her moment in the sun. I didn't care what they thought, I would bring Emily. I wouldn't put her up front with the others, wouldn't allow her screaming or behaviors to ruin the day, but I wanted her there.

This was also likely the moment I decided I was not going to sugarcoat things; I was not going to cower or kowtow to those who did not support what I was seeking for my daughter. I would do my best to be cordial, but I was tired of the pushback. I was ready to be aggressive in pursuing educational opportunities that others were intent on denying her. If making enemies was what it took, then so be it. Emily's life counted.

ON THE DAY of the preschool graduation everyone gathered in an outside area with hay bales, sawdust, and a split-rail fence.

All the parents had their video cameras whizzing; the kids were dressed up. The school was located in a section of Tarzana zoned for horses. One of the families supplied a pony and most of the kids took turns riding the pony and squealing.

Tom and I showed up with Emily and we kept to the back of the crowd. Twenty or so of Emily's classmates attended with their parents, siblings, and grandparents to cheer them on. A ceremony commenced with the kids wearing construction-paper mortarboards, receiving little pretend diplomas. I was worried Emily would start screaming and disrupt things, nervous that she'd draw unwanted attention. This was an act of defiance on my part, being in a place they had specifically asked us not to be. Frankly, I'm still a little ashamed of myself that I didn't more vigorously advocate for her, that I only protested in this small way. Still, I didn't want to shoot ourselves in the foot. This had been the only preschool that had accepted her, and they'd been nice.

The day unfolded; Emily didn't disrupt anything. Her name wasn't called out and she didn't receive a diploma, but she was present and we congratulated our daughter on completing preschool. It was on that day that my advocacy was born.

A FEW WEEKS later, I awoke at 3:00 a.m., unable to sleep. This happened a lot.

I was in a state of chronic anxiety. Every morning, I woke not knowing which child I would greet. Some days Emily was a joy to be around, inquisitive, engaged, cheerful. Other days, she screamed and cried, hit herself and scratched us from morning until night over upsets we could neither predict nor fully mitigate. This stress rubbed off. Whenever Emily got upset, Tom and I moved into shut-down mode. We did only what had to be done to move through the hours until we could finally sleep. When she was happy, though, we were great. You could take our temperature, as individuals and as a couple, by Emily's mood.

This night, I woke fretting, mulling over how to solve any number of the problems we were facing. I worried if I'd signed her up with the right therapies and with the right practitioners. Perhaps there were interventions I hadn't yet explored. I was concerned that my law practice was suffering with my attention so splintered. My brain ran through them all, obsessing.

My quest on Emily's behalf had already taken me across the whole of Los Angeles County, to seminars, schools, lectures, and presentations. This particular night, as my mental search engine powered through options, I remembered the speech therapist I'd met at Villa Esperanza, Alicia Elliott. Suddenly, she was like a bright light in a dark tunnel. I jumped out of bed, found my purse and dug through it, rummaging for the card I'd shoved into it months ago. I held it in my hand, convinced *this* was what we needed to do. We'd hire Alicia Elliott. Privately, not through Villa Esperanza. That would do it. I woke up Tom to tell him my brainstorm.

"Go back to sleep, Valerie. We'll talk about it later."

The next morning, I felt a spark of optimism that had been missing for far too long. I finally had the answer.

WHEN I RAISED the idea with Tom the next day, though, his response was lukewarm. The dynamic between us often put

55

us on opposite sides. I was always looking for something new to try and see if it worked, while he was always cautious, wanting to follow the tried-and-true path. Through all the weariness, we fought a lot. Still, I was convinced for the first time in ages that I was on the right path. At that point, Tom hadn't met Alicia. If he only met her, he'd feel her magnetism, he'd see it my way. I was certain.

I'd been in contact with her and she'd reassured me she had time to work with Emily.

THE NEXT TIME Tom and I met with Doreen for an update meeting, I brought up my concerns.

"I told you," Doreen said, "we will add in the speech therapy with my own therapists. We can do all that. There's no need to bring in someone else."

"I don't think the current program is working."

"That's because she needs even more hours. So far, we've been working with her, let's see . . ." She consulted her notes. "Twenty-five hours a week. As you pointed out, she's not improving. Clearly, the time we've allotted is not sufficient. We need to increase it."

"Increase it?" I was flabbergasted. Emily hated every moment of the behavioral therapy. I didn't want to inflict yet more on her.

"She needs seventy hours," Doreen said.

"That's crazy. She's a child. She needs a life."

Even Tom was taken aback. He looked pained.

"That kind of intensity is what she needs," Doreen continued. "Better yet, she needs someone to be with her twenty-four/seven to talk to her, to direct her."

"She needs more than behavior modification," I argued. "She needs to learn to communicate."

"Who besides us is going to be able to help her in this intensive way?"

"Alicia Elliott."

"No, she won't. She won't be able to give her the kinds of hours she needs."

"I've spoken with her. She will."

Doreen was not happy. "What we're doing is what Emily needs. And here you are, looking to replace these therapies? She needs someone to be talking with her, working with her every waking moment of her life."

I felt scolded but determined. We left that meeting with no resolution. I was exasperated.

I TOOK UP the argument baton with Tom later that night. "We need to move her to Alicia Elliott. This is the best option."

"Why now, when we have all this set up, after all the time and energy we've invested?" He, too, was deflated and frustrated, but also under Doreen's sway, as though he had chosen her over me. It made me mad.

"Because it's not helping her. Do you see her getting any closer to speaking to us? Do you see her improving any more? Because I don't."

"Maybe she's not able to."

"How do we know that? We haven't given this a try."

"What we have in place is good. Let's not fix things that aren't broken. We're making progress. I'm just as frustrated as you. Still, changing course now doesn't makes sense."

"Doreen said she needed seventy hours a week. Did you hear her? That's insane."

Tom agreed. "We're already on behavior overload. Still . . . I don't know about this."

"Well, I *do* know." I had reached my limit. In my bones I knew that Alicia was the way we needed to go. I was ready to stake everything on that knowledge, even my marriage.

"Alicia Elliott can give Emily what she needs," I said. "The timing is perfect. Since it's summer, many of her regular clients have relinquished their spots. She can make room for Emily."

"The behavioral therapy is what Dr. Sigman recommended," Tom countered. "Why can't we just see it through?"

"It's been three years!" I was now shouting. "Besides, Alicia's been successful with other autistic kids. She's moved them toward communication."

I worked myself into a frenzy. I was so upset and concerned. In those days, I was in tears all the time. I wasn't completely irrational, I know, but I wasn't the most reasonable person on the planet, either. I can be very headstrong when I set my mind to something, not leaving much room to negotiate. The skills that served me well as an attorney didn't exactly make me easy to live with.

"Say what you want, Tom, I'm doing this."

The truth was, I was obsessed with Emily, with everything about her, and in that moment, I wanted Tom to simply say, *Great. Let's do it.* I was baiting him, trying to get his attention, desperately trying to wrest a different response from him. I wasn't so much frustrated with *him* as I was with the problem, but I needed proof he was fully on my side. I wasn't being fair; I can see that now. Still, I demanded his full-throated affirmation and nothing short of that. When he wavered, I gave him an ultimatum.

"Either we make this change, or I'm taking Emily and leaving you."

My parents read to me all the time, always before bed but at other times, too, like if we were waiting at a doctor's office or there was a quiet patch in the day. Mom or Dad would pull me close and read very clearly, following along with a finger on each of the words. Mom read in a distinct voice and always picked age-appropriate stories. She didn't always read the same one book over and over again. Sometimes I would push her to stop and she'd tell me how important it was.

Being read to was a beautiful comfort first, and something of a tool second. It contributed greatly to my writing but also to listening and receiving information. It gave me long bursts of material to focus on. I was able to hear the stories again, which taught me the significance of a story, that they are good more than once and meant to be revisited.

I can remember the books' smells. All books have a smell. Different books have different smells. Some books I liked just for the smell.

There was a blue book with stars and the night sky that I'd ask for over and over. I'd go get the book and hand it to Mom. I loved that book. As I got older, I wanted to hear stories about kids growing up in different places or of a different race, kids experiencing struggles I could not know. Plus poetry. I think I favored poetry even early on.

Language always was interesting to me, often even more so than the story. Sometimes, the story was already known to me, but I would pay attention because I liked the language. I learned the way to work words around. For example, rhymes or word choices would be what captivated me more than the actual story.

There are special words, I discovered. The word "spectacular," for instance, has always been a dance in my ears. And I love to hear words that shouldn't rhyme, but then they do.

All those years, I was rearranging words in my head. I would hear the words in my head even if I couldn't say them.

6

Back when Emily was diagnosed at age two, I had immediately started my research to understand what we were dealing with, still convinced that with a forceful effort to interrupt the disorder, we'd have Emily back on track by the time she started kindergarten. We'd throw all the time and money needed to change the trajectory of this disorder and we'd simply make it go away. I can see now that was magical thinking. Over the two and a half decades I've spent learning about autism and living with Emily, my thinking and understanding about autism have evolved.

Initially, we were told that autism was a disorder of the central nervous system, which meant, essentially, that all aspects of her body were impacted. The National Institute of Mental Health calls autism spectrum disorder (ASD) "a developmental disorder that affects communication and behavior." Although autism can be diagnosed at any age, it is said to be a "developmental disorder" because symptoms generally appear in the first two years of life. When Emily was diagnosed, autism was characterized as a spectrum disorder as there were so many variants, from those who were severely impacted to those who were less so.

In order to diagnose Emily, doctors simply observed her. Though the diagnosis was based on the criteria laid out in the *Diagnostic and Statistical Manual of Mental Health Disorders*, none of the doctors we consulted at that time mentioned that volume. The DSM-5, the current iteration, maintains the breakdown of eligibility based on communication and behavioral deficits, but parses the basis for eligibility in a manner different from the version of the DSM in play in 1993.

I don't recall that any kind of standardized test was ever used to assess Emily, even when she saw Dr. John Menkes, well known for his definitive work, *Child Neurology*. While observation is still the main basis for diagnosing, standardized tests are now routinely used.

In many ways, we were then in the Dark Ages when it comes to understanding this disorder. (As far as I'm concerned, we're still in the Dark Ages with this disability, but that's another story.) Since her diagnosis, a lot has changed. Still, even with all the reading I've done and the advances in understanding that have come along, it's clear to me that the initial information we were provided was correct. In our experience, autism came down to issues with the central nervous system, and the best way to diagnose and characterize the condition was through noting disturbances with the motor functions—impairment to speech, social interaction, and eye contact.

The Centers for Disease Control and Prevention (CDC) reports that people with ASD often have problems with social, emotional, and communication skills. They might repeat certain behaviors and might not want change in their daily activities. Many with ASD also have different ways of learning, paying attention, or reacting to things. Signs of ASD begin during early childhood and typically last throughout a person's life. Children or adults with ASD might:

- not point at objects to show interest (for example, not point at an airplane flying over)
- not look at objects when another person points at them
- have trouble relating to others or not have an interest in other people at all
- avoid eye contact and want to be alone
- have trouble understanding other people's feelings or talking about their own feelings
- prefer not to be held or cuddled, or might cuddle only when they want to
- appear to be unaware when people talk to them, but respond to other sounds
- be very interested in people, but not know how to talk, play, or relate to them
- repeat or echo words or phrases said to them, or repeat words or phrases in place of normal language
- have trouble expressing their needs using typical words or motions
- not play "pretend" games (for example, not pretend to "feed" a doll)
- repeat actions over and over again
- have trouble adapting when a routine changes
- have unusual reactions to the way things smell, taste, look, feel, or sound
- lose skills they once had (for example, stop saying words they were using)

As I pointed out earlier, the signs of autism we observed in Emily included the loss of and/or failure to develop speech, babbling, and social skills. Her beginning efforts at speech soon evaporated—sounding out the "B" in the Burger King sign; or saying to Tom, "I go play"—as did her eye contact with us.

Like many children with autism, she also engaged in repetitive behaviors like flapping her hands, rocking, or spinning, or making unusual sounds constantly. These are often referred to as "self-stimulatory behaviors" or "stims." Some believe that stims satisfy a sensory need for the individual.

Emily also demonstrated a great resistance to even minor changes in her routine and surroundings, a quality that behavioral modification was intended to address. For example, she preferred a certain route when I drove to Target and became agitated if I took a different way. She resisted playing with toys and had to be coaxed into doing so. At times, she screamed at sudden loud noises like coughing or sneezing, and would gag at strong smells like bleach. I learned that not all children with autism show *all* the signs, and many children who *don't* have autism show a few of them.

Over time, I have had the opportunity to work with Deborah Budding, a neuropsychologist who specializes in sensorimotor development and subcortical contributions to neurodevelopmental and psychiatric disorders, including autism. Recently, at Emily's request we met with her so that she could answer Emily's questions regarding the disorder. She provided us with a definition of autism that was a little different from what we'd initially understood, and yet it rang true. She said that autism is a motor/movement disorder that affects the timing and quality of movements, including those involved in communication. "Movement is everything," Dr. Budding said. "There is nothing that we do that does not involve movement in some way."

Further, Dr. Budding does not believe autism to be an illness, per se. She acknowledged that with autism there is often comorbidity with medical illnesses, like epilepsy or ADHD*; this has been well documented and makes sense because autism is a function of motor limitation, and it affects just about every part of a person's being. However, she believes that much of what may look like "illness" is really a result of the nervous system's dysfunction, including poorly supported communication. If one accepts that autism is not an illness, then it is not a disease to be cured but more a state of being that requires varying degrees of support given the world we live in. For example, people with autism may benefit from being trained to use typed communication, and though some are able to access speech, they may need speech therapy to do so more fluently. Other supports they would benefit from include assistance in developing daily living skills like grooming, home care, using public transportation, and navigating the ever-changing landscape of the world we live in.

I agree with Dr. Budding that autism is not a disease or illness at all. The way I see it, it's a condition made up of certain neurological challenges, a function of brain synapses that fail to connect adequately, and which results in physical

---

* Autism is a disorder that can affect the entire body. According to the National Center for Biotechnology (NCBI), "adults with autism had significantly increased rates of all major psychiatric disorders including depression, anxiety, bipolar disorder, obsessive-compulsive disorder, schizophrenia, and suicide attempts. Nearly all medical conditions were significantly more common in adults with autism, including immune conditions, gastrointestinal and sleep disorders, seizure, obesity, dyslipidemia, hypertension, and diabetes. Rarer conditions, such as stroke and Parkinson's disease, were also significantly more common among adults with autism."

attributes like an odd gait and arms that don't move when the person walks. Fundamentally, it's a neurological motor issue affecting motor skills, and most definitely not a psychological disorder.

One of the most puzzling phenomena associated with ASD is when children seem to regress developmentally—Emily's loss of emerging speech, for example, or her early imaginative play that seemed to disappear. The assertion that such regression occurs is not shared by all the experts. Many claim that about one-third of young children with ASD lose some skills during the preschool period, usually speech, but sometimes also nonverbal communication, social or play skills. No one really knows the nature or mechanism involved in this so-called regression.

While Tom and I initially thought we were witnessing Emily's preschool regression, the reality seen from today's vantage point is this: When we look back at early photos and videos of Emily, it's pretty clear that she presented with many elements of the disability long before she was formally diagnosed—we just didn't recognize them. Maybe she didn't really regress at all and we simply didn't comprehend what we were seeing.

Indeed, shortly after Emily was diagnosed, I was told by a developmental pediatrician that experts were looking closer at the movement of infants in their cribs; they believed they could see early warning signs of autism in very young infants. It really is a question of knowing what to look for, this doctor said. Perhaps what appears to be regression in these young children is misunderstood.

Either way, as we've seen, Emily presented with all the markers of classic autism that had been identified in 1993. She toe-walked, and failed to make eye contact. As a baby, she made guttural, animal noises but these sounds changed over the years. Now those early sounds are gone, and though she still does not talk much, she makes near-constant noises, as if she is perpetually talking to herself. Her sounds are a kind of singsong cadence that's somewhat like a background melody. She's learned to be quiet when needed, in a classroom, say, but the ongoing sounds she makes are often when she is not under pressure to restrain them.

Emily will still engage in self-stimulatory activity when she is anxious, overwhelmed, excited, happy. From what I've come to understand, the "stimming" that autistic individuals engage in is really not so different from some behaviors that many of us neurotypical folks do and has the same intended purpose. Biting your nails, tapping a pencil, twirling your hair: these are all activities that may help to calm or focus you and are all a form of stimming. What sets apart autistic stimming, though, is simply what is culturally tolerated.

There's no question that some stims can be quite extreme and legitimately upsetting or even frightening to other people. Meltdowns—which are a function of a person's system being flooded or physically overwhelmed by sensory input—can be alarming in their intensity and duration. Deborah Budding makes a distinction between a tantrum, which is an effort to control others through acting out, and a meltdown, which is when a person is overtaken physiologically by some event in the environment. A person might learn how to rein in tantrums, but meltdowns are another story, often outside the person's realm of control.

IN 1993, WHEN Emily was diagnosed, all resources for remediation pointed to applied behavior analysis—what we'd been doing with Doreen and her team of behaviorists. ABA was then the most researched and commonly used intervention, the gold standard. We were told, like many other families at the time, that the only way out of autism was to provide very intensive ABA therapy, up to forty hours a week.

Many families I have met and spoken with since then, though certainly not all, believe that ABA created a negative experience for their child. In fact, many young adults who were subjected to ABA have shared their experience from a personal point of view and feel similarly. Emily has written of her own frustrations with the ABA therapy, noting that doing mundane tasks like touching her nose on command did little to help her. As with anything, though, everyone has a different experience.

I have my own perspective on the final results of the ABA therapy. I believe that because in therapy she was always responding to the demands of another person—*touch your nose, touch your head, come here, put the toy there*—Emily learned to always be in a reactive mode. She was never taught to be proactive. As a result, she developed a fear of initiating action, a personality attribute that has remained with her. To this day, she won't ask for a snack when hungry. She rarely asserts herself verbally and originates very few actions on her own. She rarely if ever requests or demands anything of anyone. I believe this stems from the ABA.

Meanwhile, the speech and occupational therapies we pursued had mixed results. School- and clinic-based occupational therapy, which addressed Emily's fine and gross motor skills and issues with her internal timing, were helpful. However, the most significant contribution to Emily's development came from a specialized gymnastics program, BIG

FUN, that Emily attended from seven until about twelve. Gene Hurwin, an occupational therapist who developed the program, wanted to address the gross and fine motor issues of autistic children through gymnastics, and particularly their neurotiming—the synchronization of neural impulses within key brain networks for cognitive, communicative, sensory, and motor performance. His approach included work on the balance beam, tumbling, climbing apparatus, and trampoline to help children synchronize their bodies and minimize those aspects of their movements that were off by just a second or two from their neurotypical peers—an awkward gait, say, or arms that did not swing when walking. Though the program also focused on sensory integration—an effort to integrate the sensory sensitivity of the autistic child with environmental noises—Emily experienced limited progress in this area. From my perspective, one session with Gene was worth five sessions of generic occupational therapy because movement and timing were key issues with Emily's limitations. By addressing those disconnects, we gained the most progress.

The speech therapy services that we also sought, on the other hand, clearly did not help in the ways we'd hoped.

All these observations come in hindsight and are limited to my experience with Emily. There's a saying in the autistic community: "If you've met one autistic person, you've met one autistic person." There's such a range of behaviors and experiences that to generalize in any way is to do a grave disservice. Emily has certain skills and abilities that other autistic people do not, while others may have skills and abilities Emily does not. It's all so varied. So of course, what would help her may be different from what would help someone else.

To get a better sense of where Emily falls in the continuum of those who are considered to be autistic, I recently asked Nancy Wolf, MD, a specialist in child and adolescent psychiatry and one of Emily's doctors who has seen Emily since she was thirteen, to give her assessment of Emily.

"When I first saw her, my immediate impression was that I thought that there was something else going on besides autism, and that I was looking at somebody who was acutely intelligent. And yet she wasn't able to answer me, and she was just making noises. She had way too attentive and intelligent a look for her not to be much more aware than she was credited to be, or at least having read notes of prior doctors and such.

"She did have this aphasia"—the loss of ability to express speech, usually caused by brain damage. Still, "I thought that she had much more understanding and comprehension of things than we were really able to prove, or were aware of."

As evidence of this comprehension, Dr. Wolf pointed out Emily's attendance in school.

"When she went to school with an aide, she was able to take fairly sophisticated courses. I thought to myself, if she wasn't comprehending any of this, she would get up and leave or have a tantrum, because she was prone to tantrums. She wouldn't have been able to stay in the classrooms because she would have been stimming so much. She would have made a lot more noises and been so disruptive in the classes. They wouldn't have been able to keep her there. But the fact was that she *did* attend school and was anxious to attend school, and wanted to be there." That desire, Dr. Wolf implied, indicated a lot.

"Her speech is really kind of odd. It would be very gruff.

It was really hard for her to even verbalize those kinds of inputs." Still, Emily was "way too appropriate in the way she responded. There were certain questions I could ask, and she would respond with a correct yes or no each time and was accurate.

"'Is your name Emily?'

"'Yes.'

"'Is your name Susan?'

"'No.'"

Dr. Wolf varied the questions, but Emily always had an applicable, accurate response.

"She *did* have enormous physical control challenges," the doctor recalled. "Like tantrums, and if she stayed in one place too long, she'd become restless. I saw what you and Tom must have had to deal with at home. That would cause a lot of friction."

As far as her diagnosis goes, Dr. Wolf said to look at the DSM-IV and -5 as systems of categorization. "They're like Chinese restaurant menus, two from column A and three from column B, and you have a diagnosis. . . . What I was saying, is that a diagnosis is a phenomenological entity. It doesn't explain why somebody has what they have. They have [it], it just shows you what you see."

In discussing Emily's case, she listed the evidence.

"She stims, making unusual motions with her hands in front of her eyes. These are things people with autism do to calm themselves. She has the hypersensitivity to a lot of stimuli" that's often seen with autism. "She has impaired communication and impaired social relationships" that are also common.

"So she fits whatever criteria is necessary to call her

autistic," but that diagnosis doesn't speak to whether she has this phenomenon due to brain damage, or whether she stims because she has an allergy, or anything else. "Could her symptoms be caused by variable diseases? Technically, they could."

Given the restaurant menu approach to choose from, Dr. Wolf said she technically fits the criteria as listed in the DSM to classify her as autistic.

There can be no assumptions made within autism. We're not all alike. Not at all. There is no textbook, as they say, no clear description of the word 'autism' that identifies all of us. If you ask me, it's worse a crime than stereotyping to think of us as all being similar.

I am one of the lucky ones. I had people who saw the person I was. I had people who knew that I was not as cognitively small as my speech was determined to portray.

I also know that I can't speak for every autistic person either, because if I did, my words would make me just as guilty as those who stuff us all into the same box.

Which brings me to one example: the assumption so often made that all autistic people are extremely literal. But I can write figuratively and in metaphor and abstractly, and in turn I can hear these things and think around the words to uncover their true meaning within a sentence.

When it comes to autistic people, it's best not to make assumptions. Many of us have skills that might surprise you. None of us is the same.

7

A group of kids led by Alicia Elliott's partner were singing "Baby Beluga," a nursery song made famous by Raffi, when the three of us arrived at her office.

> Baby beluga in the deep blue sea
> Swim so wild and you swim so free
> Heaven above and the sea below
> And a little white whale on the go

In no time, Emily was trying to follow along and enunciate the words.

Tom had come with me to visit the group class on a Saturday. When I'd issued my ultimatum, I hadn't thought through the implications of my words; I didn't have a plan. I loved him, and I was lashing out in a moment of anger and exasperation. I'd wanted to force the issue, to make him pay attention. I'd been so obsessed with this new plan, I was ready to bulldoze my way there. The fact that he was willing to give my suggestion a try despite my strong-arm tactics, and he didn't just throw up his hands in exasperation with me, was a testament to the strength of our marriage.

Saturday was the one day a week when many of Alicia's private clients all came together, so the room was filled to bursting with a half dozen kids and their parents. The minute we walked in, the happiness and joy were palpable, kids singing, parents relaxed, laughter in the air. Fun was taking place. After all the time we'd spent with the dour behaviorists, awash in their seriousness and data collection along with Emily's vocal and pained resistance to them, this was such a relief. Kids here were enjoying themselves. The whole timbre of the experience was filled with ease and delight. Even Emily was glad to be there. My shoulders relaxed for the first time in weeks.

I looked over at my husband and saw him tapping his foot to the "Baby Beluga" song, caught up in the joy of the room. He was being won over. Thank goodness. I would have sacrificed my relationship with Tom on the altar of Emily, and our marriage would have suffered as a result.

I've talked with a lot of parents of special needs kids and many of them end up divorcing—the majority, in fact—because it puts such a strain on the relationship. As a couple, you stop having the kind of social life you used to have. While I can't speak for everyone, certainly our hopes and dreams, as well as our plans, were impacted by our constant considerations for Emily. So much of our life stood still. Everything in our orbit revolved around Emily. Parents often have to choose between their spouse and their child, a Sophie's choice no one should ever have to make. Though Tom and I don't always see eye to eye on how to get Emily the care she needs, our commitment to our daughter as our first priority has been unwavering from the start. Still, it took a toll and made for some unhappy moments.

Other relationships were strained, too. We were not native Angelenos and had no entrenched long-standing relationships in the area. It's different when you live as an adult in the same place you grew up, where people have known you over the course of a lifetime and you have a shared history; you can rely on them to help you out. Having no extended family in the area didn't help. Still, we did our best to have a social life, celebrating Emily's birthday with a party at our home with her friends from school and our own friends. We often had small dinner parties. Milestones—her graduations, Tom's appointment to the bench—were all fully celebrated. I did my best to punctuate important events.

Over time, though, almost all our old friends drifted away—we had so little in common with them given our new reality. Our newer friends were people in the same boat, parents also raising disabled children. Socializing even within this new group was limited. We were never able to exhale around people, never knew what Emily might do, what behavior or screaming might interrupt an event. We didn't try to hide her; we took her to parties and other social outings, but it was stressful. I didn't know when or how I'd have to do a lot of explaining.

On those nights when Tom and I could get away, we tried to connect with others, looking to escape the drumbeat of our daily life if only for a few hours; still, we remained socially isolated.

I'm reminded of Maslow's hierarchy of needs. We were stuck at the bottom rungs of that pyramid, trying to get the basic physiological and safety needs met for ourselves and our daughter. This meant little time or energy left over for higher-order satisfactions like friendships, social outings, and intimacy with others. We were just making it on a survival basis.

Now, at Alicia's office, though, we both felt a moment of reprieve. As we watched Emily with the other kids in the room, we noticed that both Alicia and her partner were exceptionally attuned to the needs of the children. It was wonderful how nurturing the environment was, how these women led them in songs, in games, remaining playful and encouraging throughout. No scolding. None of the zero-sum game of behaviorists—*If you don't do what we ask, you won't get the treat*. Everyone was playful and learning through games and amusement, not via withheld reinforcement.

In no time, Tom was on board. While we'd greatly appreciated the behaviorists' help over the years, we couldn't be happier to no longer be locked in the behavior modification shackles. I was so sick of the tiny M&M's, the cajoling, the bits of cookie, the reams of data, the constant presence of strangers in our home, the weekly meetings. And, most of all, Emily's resistance to the process. Now, with Alicia in place as Emily's go-to therapy, I had to figure out kindergarten.

I'D RECENTLY LEARNED that I could hire an attorney to advocate for Emily,[*] someone who might be able to compel the school district to reimburse us for some of these very expensive therapies, as well as for some of the costs of the Montessori preschool. The school district could also give her access to classrooms specifically devoted to special needs children.

Having a lawyer in our corner would be a benefit, and

---

[*] Non-attorney advocates can also provide this service to parents. But as cases progress, a lawyer may be needed.

Doreen had long suggested an attorney to us, but I hadn't followed up. First, I'd needed to make some mistakes.

WHEN WE'D INITIALLY been looking into public preschool options for Emily—before we found the Montessori school—I'd come across one that had interested me.

"I'd like to enroll my daughter in this preschool," I explained to the school office personnel.

"To be considered, we need to have an IEP in place on her."

"What's that?" I asked.

Looking back, I can't believe that it took so long for me to get clued in. I quickly learned that an IEP is an individualized education plan, a legal document under United States law that is developed for each public school child[*] in the US who needs a special education. This plan is created by a team composed of the child's parent(s) and district personnel who are knowledgeable about the child. It lays out the services the school district needs to supply in order for the child to be provided a "free and appropriate public education," otherwise known as a FAPE.

I found out how to get the IEP process started. Many assessments later, we sat in a room at a local school, eight pairs of eyes facing me and Tom across the table as the assessments from the district's employees were presented at Emily's initial IEP team meeting. It was agreed that Emily qualified

---

[*] A school district is also required to offer an IEP to students attending private schools if they otherwise qualify. It amounts to a contract with the family, and serves to detail the basis of eligibility, the classroom placement, and services that the district is offering to address a particular student's needs, at least as seen from the district's perspective.

under the category of "autism"* as well as under "speech and language impairment." The school district offered her placement in a special day preschool class, designed solely for autistic students. We were thrilled.

WHEN I PULLED up for her first day at this assigned preschool, I noticed that the classroom she'd been offered was not part of the school proper. It was housed in a trailer (described charitably by the district as a "bungalow") on the blacktop on the farthest perimeter of the school property. This was a way to keep autistic kids segregated.

I took her in and introduced her to the teacher and the aide, as well as the other eleven students. Instead of just dropping Emily off, I stuck around to see what was happening.

From day one, I could see the teacher and aide had no clear organization for the class and its curriculum. All the kids were acting out. Rather than learning from her peers who were doing what we hoped Emily would do—be attentive in class; learn to identify letters, numbers, and colors; engage with her classmates and teachers in a healthy, appropriate manner—the environment inflamed already problem behaviors. Her screaming, stimming, and self-harm became more rampant. The only thing Emily liked about the preschool were the times she could stare out the window at the neurotypical children having fun during recess. She was

---

* Eligibility for development of an IEP is determined following initial assessment by a school district. The current categories for eligibility under the federal law include autism, other health impairment, intellectual impairment, specific learning disability, emotional disturbance, speech or language impairment, visual impairment, deafness, hearing impairment, orthopedic impairment, traumatic brain injury, or Multiple Disabilities.

content then and quieted down. The school viewed this negatively and documented her window gazing as evidence of just how distractible she was.

Indeed, when I next came to visit the class, I found a piece of cardboard taped to the window Emily looked out of. The action was intended to help focus her—the teacher was annoyed she didn't have Emily's full attention—but it only forced her deeper inside herself.

The final straw came when I entered the classroom and found that Robert, one of the boys in her class who was extremely challenged behaviorally, was boxed in with movable walls inside the confines of the classroom.

"What's going on?" I asked.

"His behaviors are too much," the harried teacher said as she tried to deal with the dozen kids running around her, not listening, screaming, and rocking. "I don't want any of the others imitating his bad behavior."

This environment clearly wasn't helping Emily. I realized then just how different one person's view of what an "appropriate" education can be. That was the end for me. That's how we ended up at the Montessori school in Tarzana.

To understand fully my advocacy on Emily's behalf at this time, it's important to know the context. Emily was born in 1991, when laws had recently changed to be on her side. Prior to this time, things had been different. Access to educational services for the disabled was codified back in 1975 when President Gerald Ford signed into law the Education for All Handicapped Children Act. This act obligated all states that accepted money from the federal government to provide equal access to education for children with disabilities. Prior to this time, these services were not available in all states. A later amendment required states to provide services to the families of children born with disabilities from the time of the child's birth.

In 1986, President Reagan signed into law the Handicapped Children's Protection Act, which gave parents of children with disabilities the right to increased input in the development of their child's individual education plan. Finally, in January 1990—less than two years before Emily was born—autism and traumatic brain injury were added as categories of disability that the school districts were required to serve.

Over time, I wised up to the IEP game and realized I'd need an attorney to help us figure out how to maximize the benefits to Emily. As kindergarten loomed, I hired a well-respected advocate who'd worked tirelessly in California to change the laws around educational access for disabled children. She had a reputation for being a bulldog. We needed her in our corner.

Working with this attorney, we learned the range of possible services available under federal and California law. That's not to say that our advocacy in getting those services was easy or the outcome a sure thing. The burden remained on us to demonstrate that these services (speech, occupational, and/or behavioral therapy) would, in fact, benefit her. The obligation to prove our case continued on a yearly basis. In fact, we had to sue the local school district repeatedly to obtain what had been established as Emily's right under the Individuals with Disabilities Education Act: a free and appropriate public education.

BY THE TIME kindergarten rolled around, I saw my expectation that our early intervention would solve the autism challenge was not going to happen. She was nowhere near ready for a regular classroom: behaviorally, socially, or emotionally. She was clearly autistic. Symptoms we'd seen when she was younger were now in full bloom.

Like with the preschool search, I'd already taken her to four or five private schools to seek acceptance in their kindergarten classrooms. Once they watched how she walked, her reactions, how she dealt with people, the school administrators recognized she had way too many needs for the school to meet. We saw it, too. Every one of those schools said no, even the most unconventional one. Emily could not function independently; we could all see it. By this time, though, we'd had five years to get used to the idea that improvements would not occur on the timeline I'd initially anticipated. Nor would they ever.

I'm used to operating in a world where, if I set my mind to something, I can accomplish it. Now, this was a new experience, not getting what I wanted and being told no. It changed me as a person. I became very patient with Emily.

LOOKING FOR A special education kindergarten, I happened upon Mrs. Morrow's K-1 "aphasia" classroom in Northridge at a public school. Immediately, I felt at home. For one, Mrs. Morrow's classroom was part of the actual school building; I was unwilling to go along with the segregation of disabled students that was commonly practiced on elementary school campuses. Mrs. Morrow was an actual speech and language pathologist who taught language-challenged children in this mixed-grade special ed class. She was a professional who understood the needs of these kids.

The room was organized, the walls decorated in cheery colors. An aide working with the kids was focused on each individual. Mrs. Morrow spoke to the eight or so kids in the class with the utmost kindness and respect. The adult-to-child ratio was much better than anything else I'd seen, and each child was happily occupied. I'd found the needle in the haystack.

The minute I got back into my car, I called our attorney.

"I can't believe this class. This is like the best in the world. Who knew there were classes like this?" I gushed. "Can we get in?" I asked.

"We'll do our best," she said.

EMILY STARTED KINDERGARTEN in that class in the fall. I took a picture on the first day, insistent on marking this as a milestone well known to the parents of neurotypical kids. Each morning, I drove Emily to school, and when I picked her up in the early afternoon we sprinted across town to Alicia's office, adding a sixty-two-mile round-trip drive on top of the extensive school commute. Emily worked with Alicia from three to six each afternoon, five days a week, even longer on Saturdays.

I still had my private law practice and became a have-briefcase-will-travel attorney to keep up with Emily's schedule. Either I'd bring all my work files, my car phone (handheld cell phones would come later), and my laptop with me, and basically practice law from my car while she received therapy, or I'd drop her off and Tom, who then worked in

Monterey Park, east of Los Angeles, would swing by to pick her up at the end of the day. On the days Tom picked her up, I had just enough time to rush home and prepare some kind of dinner before they arrived. If the pace we'd been keeping previously had been hard, this was grueling. Every day was a new challenge, wondering how in the world we were going to manage.

"THERE'S THIS COMPUTER program we could try," Alicia suggested. One of the reasons I liked her was that she was on the forefront of what was happening in the world of autism treatment. She'd hear about an intervention that might benefit Emmy and would suggest it to us. If Alicia suggested it, it was worth pursuing. This was 1998 and using computers and technology in this capacity was fairly new.

We signed Emily up for Fast ForWord, a recently developed computer program designed to change neural passages in the brain, particularly those around the phonemic endings of words. Words like "phone" and "photo" can be confused by someone like Emily because the ending of the word can be lost, thus changing the meaning. This confusion is attributed to an auditory processing disorder (different from a hearing loss, which had been suggested by the music teacher when Emily was a toddler), another issue secondary to the overall neurological compromise.

Emily sat in front of a computer screen wearing headphones and had to answer questions. *Show me the picture of the girl <u>watching</u> a cow*, the program asked, providing a number of illustrations to choose from. Then, *Show me the picture of a girl <u>washing</u> a cow*. Emily used a mouse to indicate her choice. Over time, her ability to tell the difference between the words and to better understand what was being said to her improved.

At Alicia's suggestion, she also used Interactive Metronome, designed to train Emily's body and brain to work together better. As I had come to understand, autism manifests in a number of ways, including the speech and language difficulties we were currently addressing, as well as the behavioral issues we'd previously addressed through the behavior modification. There were also body control challenges, manifested in an autistic person as an unsteady or uneven gait, or in an imbalanced walk in which the person may not swing their arms at all, or may do so with off-beat timing—not the smooth right-foot/left-arm, balanced walk most of us exhibit. As I read up on the subject, I learned that these body control issues were evidence of a blip with Emily's neurotiming. To help correct this, an actual metronome was utilized. Emily clapped her hands or tapped her foot to a beat, working to get better at matching various pulses over repeated sessions. The idea was to stimulate the growth of connections in her brain to help it work more efficiently and to be more organized, much like she was doing with Gene Hurwin. Doing so, we'd hoped, would improve her focus, her ability to decipher information. It might further aid her ability to read, the ease of her movements, and help her to control her impulsive or aggressive behaviors.

Each of the suggested therapies came with a hefty price tag, but every time Alicia approached us with a new possibility, we said yes. If there was some chance that the proposed therapy might help, we wanted it. Some worked better than others. We said yes not only because a proffered therapy might change something for Emily, but also because for the hour or so of a given intervention, someone else was in charge of Emily. Tom and I got a brief respite.

Alicia is a very determined person. That was clear from the time I met her. There was a sense that she understood me and wanted to help me get as much expression as she knew was equal to all that I had in my mind. I don't know how much my mom told Alicia before we met, but she understood me. Her goal was to help me express at least my basic wants and needs. But she also knew that, even at my young age, there was more to me. She recognized my intelligence and individuality and respected it.

For instance, if she wanted to know which book I wanted to read, she didn't just settle on a generic "book." She asked me to be specific. She wanted me to be specific with colors and details and desires; she knew I had it in me.

In working on my verbal expression and practicing articulation, we'd exchange cards with pictures. She thought maybe I was unable to hear the precise sounds of words correctly, but usually I could.

Other times, she'd say a word and want me to produce the same sound. She'd show me images of the mouth and where your tongue should go, or how your teeth should be positioned and she would do things with her hand to show or help produce a sound—it looked like sign language but was not.

I felt frustrated by the pictures of the mouth and teeth because I couldn't make mine work that way. I believe she knew that I knew the differences in meaning between two words, like washing and watching. I could say them both out loud, and in my mind, they were pronounced correctly. But to the listener—to Alicia—it sounded as if they were both the same. It was a source of frustration. I was attempting different words and not succeeding. I was not pleasing her with the outcome.

Many of the interactions, though, I did enjoy. For example, there was a game or practice in which I would be asked to hand the card to her with whatever color was asked. When I got it right, I enjoyed to see that, based on her reaction. I had done it right! And if I was wrong, she would giggle and say "Try again."

Usually, I enjoyed being at her office. Sometimes it was overwhelming because I was accustomed a quieter setting, so everyone being there particularly on Saturdays was hard at first, but I enjoyed watching the other kids and joining in as I was able to.

I was glad the behaviorists had stopped coming to our house. That was a relief. When I went to Alicia's, my home remained my home. I didn't like having them all in the house and was sick of the work they were making me do. I felt that I'd made all the progress I was going to.

8

I was bored with the classes in school. I think I was fed up a lot during that time. I had a lot of feelings sometimes, and overwhelming amount of emotions with no way to express them. There was a lot more extreme behavior on my part then. Meltdowns. I was in my head a lot. I can see now that if I'd had the ability to type or to let others know what was going on inside me, it would have helped. But I didn't. I felt tangled up inside.

The younger school years were challenging at times, but also good. Can you imagine the raging energy of kids all in one place with no awareness for people's sensitivities and the way it can affect someone like me? Also, there were times when there was too little input, people weren't explaining to me what was going on and it was sometimes confusing.

A tutor once said to me that working with me was like training a dog to write a novel. It's hard to believe but it's true. That tutor wanted to get another client and hated working with me. She was part of the school's tutoring service. She told this to a coworker with me right there. I bet she thought I couldn't *understand. I got so angry. I began to stim like crazy. I mean screaming and drooling, the works. I wanted her gone and to look bad in front of her peers and boss. I think it worked. That really made my blood boil. Because she acted like I was sub-human.*

There's another very powerful memory for me from when I was thirteen. The school special education teacher was testing my intelligence to see where to place me. He was determined that I just didn't have the capability to be in any kind of school setting. That's so vivid for me because even at the time I felt it was bullshit. But it really hurt so bad. I cried inside because it was like a death sentence. To feel that I was condemned to no education, to no advancement. I never thought I'd have another chance.

But honestly, (for the most part) I have always been treated well. I think mostly during the younger years I felt less included, but no one was mean to me. I went to other kids' birthday parties and did social things. One girl in middle school had a party at her house. I went. I am an observer more than a partaker and like to see everyone, so that's what I did there, mostly just watched the other kids. A pinata was there. I took a swing at it, but it was not my thing. I always or almost always am content to just watch and observe that way.

"This is the mouse. When you move it, it moves the cursor on the screen," Tom explained to Emily when she was about six. He'd decided to teach her to use the computer but didn't know where to begin. He didn't expect much feedback, especially not verbal, but was confident they'd figure it out together.

He started describing computers to her, hoping that

something would register. If he could get her to understand how a mouse worked and simply move it within, say, a month, he'd be doing great. It would take longer, he was sure, to teach her to open a program and actually do what she wanted.

They'd just sat down to work together in the dining room. I could hear the lesson begin.

"You can move the cursor over the symbol you want. And then, if you press down on the mouse with your fingers, it makes a 'click' and that will open the program."

Soon I heard Tom laughing from where they were working. I went over to investigate. There was Emily, having commandeered the mouse from Tom, moving the cursor, clicking icons, opening programs. There was no question: she was smart.

AS A SMALL child I showed her the basket in her room used as a clothes hamper.

"When you take off your clothes, you put them in the basket." I only had to tell her once. I have friends with kids in high school and college who still haven't fully grasped that concept.

I bought her outfits and showed her which tops went with which bottoms and how to match the colors. After matching the items a single time, from then on, she picked out her clothes and matched them on her own. Likewise, when I taught her how to wipe down a dish and load the dishwasher. It took very little instruction to get her to set the table at dinnertime.

Despite her intelligence, we still had to adjust to her

language limitations. While she couldn't communicate in the ways we did, she became very good at expressing her likes and dislikes. A frown, a shake of the head, a simple yes or no communicated a lot, and her body language was pretty doggone clear about what she deemed acceptable.

"I wish my wife could be as clear about her wants and needs as Emily is," a friend joked.

Still, we so wanted to know what she thought about, what she desired, what she felt about us and our little family, who she was inside. She remained separated from us, kept apart by this language barrier, able to share only the tiniest bit of herself with us. It saddened me, and I worried for her future.

LIFE WENT ON, Emily grew and developed, and in regular, day-to-day ways, certain self-care requirements needed tending. The dentist, for one.

When she was small, I learned about a dentist for special needs kids. Perfect. I made an appointment. I took Emily in and he had her sit in the chair.

"You know, with these kids, their arms fly about when I'm doing my work. I can't examine her properly that way." He pulled out a straitjacket and attempted to put it on her.

What the hell? I almost screamed. No one was going to put a damn straitjacket on my child! I was outraged. This was a dentist who billed himself as an expert with special needs children. Anyone with a straitjacket could terrify a child into getting her teeth cleaned, but at what cost to the child? The stigma surrounding autism was clearly alive and well. This incident showed me I'd been wise to keep her diagnosis to myself whenever possible. Let people know your child is autistic and this is what you got.

I refused to let him treat her. As we left, I declined to pay for the appointment and saw the note he put in her file. "Mother uncooperative." I didn't care. That was *not* going to happen with my daughter.

I called up my own dentist and told her the situation.

"Bring her over," she said.

The first time I went to Dr. Suzan Vigil's office with Emily, she was about five or six. To show Emily what would happen, I reclined myself on the dental chair while Emily watched.

"Open your mouth, Valerie, and I'll count and look at your teeth, clean a few of them," Dr. Suzan instructed me.

Emily watched and saw that the experience was okay; I was not being harmed. That was enough for one day.

The next appointment, three months later, Emily lay in the chair with me, her little body positioned on top of my own.

"Open your mouth, Emily, and I'll count your teeth like we did with your mom last time. I'll be touching your teeth." She did so with the metal probe. "Let's try one together so you can see what it feels like." The dentist was gentle and careful and explained absolutely everything.

Emily looked up at me to make sure it was okay and then laid her head back on my chest and opened her mouth.

We started off slowly and allowed the dental ministrations to grow incrementally.

"I'm cleaning a tooth here."

"I'm tapping one of your back teeth, now."

We saw the dentist every three months to acclimate her.

Now, at the dentist's office, when Emily's name is called, she gets up from the waiting room by herself and follows the assistant into the office and settles herself in the chair, opening her mouth, waiting for the dentist to do her work, all on her own. Time, patience, and understanding, along with letting her know what's happening, makes such a huge difference.

Having her blood drawn was another ordeal: screams, fighting back, full-on resistance. Until the day at Children's Hospital when she made known her preference. We were reasoning with her, trying to get her to straighten her arm so that the blood could be drawn from the crook of her elbow. She pointed to her inner wrist.

"You'd prefer they take the blood from there?" I asked, confused.

"Yes."

The phlebotomist agreed, and in no time Emily completely cooperated. She let them take the blood from her with no screams or tantrums.

What we saw time and again was that Emily was smart. If we could explain to her what was needed and get her to understand, we could make huge strides.

We decided early on that we weren't going to cave in to the diagnosis. My mother, like the preschool director, always said, "Children need to know what's expected of them." They were both right. Thus, we set standards for Emily and decided she would meet them. For instance, we assigned her daily chores from the time she was small, like helping to set or clear the dinner table, and taught her to eat with silverware, to put a napkin on her lap, to have manners. I saw this as my responsibility, to make sure she practiced good hygiene and knew how to dress herself. She would conduct herself with dignity in this world, I would see to it. And she did.

We also exposed Emily to as many social and cultural opportunities as we could. Our mantra was the worst that could happen was it would not work out. In this spirit, we traveled with her during spring and summer school vacations back East, as well as to Canada and the Northwest. We took her to Broadway shows. On those occasions when the activities on these trips overwhelmed her, we simply scaled back; if it meant leaving a show before it was over, so be it. We simply wanted her to take in and experience and enjoy what she could. We wanted it to work for the three of us.

BY THE TIME Emily hit first grade, she was "mainstreamed" at a public school, attending special ed classes for part of the day and joining a neurotypical class for the nonacademic parts of the curriculum. My office was nearby so I could stop in and volunteer as much as possible.

"Where's Emily?" I asked when I came to help one day.

"She's in with Mrs. Samuels," the teacher told me, indicating the general education second-grade class. "They're doing a special visit with reptiles."

I wandered through the school hallway, looking for her.

Through the IEP process and with the assistance of our attorney, the district had agreed to place her in this special ed class with a one-on-one aide. I didn't fully appreciate or understand the difference between mainstreaming and full inclusion at the time, but the idea that she'd join her neurotypical classmates in activities had been highly appealing. By having children that she might emulate in her daily experience, I hoped that she'd learn from them and develop her abilities.*

What sounded good as a concept, though, was not working out in the real world as I'd hoped. When Emily joined in the general education classroom, she wasn't really part of the class. The teacher appeared to be afraid of Emily and went to great lengths to keep her separate from the other kids. That separation pained me.

Today, though, she was with the general education kids. She was participating in the reptile visit. Great. She was joining in.

I opened the door to Mrs. Samuels's classroom, and almost screamed. There was Emily, in the middle of a group of kids, a massive python wrapped around her. The snake wound from her upper legs, over her waist and along her arms, all but covering her chest. A few inches more and it might be wrapped around her neck. I nearly lost it. Whose idea was it to have a seven-year-old wrapped up by a giant python?

My panic was overblown, but it wasn't because of Emily's reaction. She was happy as a clam. She's always liked snakes, and since many autistic individuals enjoy the feeling of being squeezed, maybe it felt good to her.† In the moment, though, I was alarmed. A python hug didn't seem like a safe

---

* The concept of mainstreaming is that students in special education classes are allowed to attend a general education classroom with neurotypical peers for a portion of the school day in nonacademic classes like art or physical education.

† Temple Grandin is well known for her theories on this.

activity. I intervened to get her out of the snake's clutches as soon as possible.

Like the snake, the idea of "mainstreaming" wasn't such a good idea, either.

What I saw during the course of the first grade was that Emily was treated as an interloper in the general education class, a visitor, someone tolerated but never fully welcomed. Mainstreaming only taunted her with what was possible, seeing the kids in the general education classroom learning and laughing and growing together. With mainstreaming, she'd forever be on the other side of a smudged window, looking in on that class and knowing she was excluded.

Meanwhile, the "academics" in her special education class, which took up the majority of the day, were busywork, and as more kids acted out, Emily learned that that misbehavior was acceptable, even expected in school.

AS THE PARENT of a child with special needs, one of the hardest things I've ever had to endure is just how mean people can be. I don't know why we as humans feel the need to step on or push down those who already face monumental challenges, but being made the butt of jokes, ostracized, and mocked is clearly part of the experience for many with autism and other developmental challenges. I wish it wasn't true, but it is.

Still, for every harsh word and cruel gesture I saw Emily receive and bounce back from, instances of surprising kindnesses and spontaneous generosity from people who knew her or were just passing by regularly floored me.

In preschool, one little boy sent her a note telling her that she was his best friend and he loved her. She still has it. A small thing, but heartfelt and lovely. That note clearly made Emily feel good.

In that "mainstreamed" first-grade class, when school let out for the Thanksgiving break, Emily came home and opened her hand to show me a rubbery plastic ball filled with water, trailing a length of rubber string. The kids called it a yo-yo ball. She also held bunched-up wrapping paper and a card with a scrawled message.

"Have a happy Thanksgiving, Emily," a young girl's letters spelled out. "You're my best friend. Love, Tracy."

Tracy was a Black girl who'd really taken a shine to Emily. Whenever I came to pick up Emily after school, she'd see me and ask, "Do you have anything for me, Mrs. Grodin?" I'd produce some candy or chocolate, whatever might be in my pocket. That little yo-yo ball gift—it cost about a buck—conveyed such heart. The kids who'd experienced stigmatization or hardship themselves were the ones who recognized Emily's challenges and gave her support.

A number of her classmates in her general education classroom had been bused in from Central Los Angeles. Mostly African American or Hispanic kids, they were often from a lower socioeconomic bracket than the kids in our upper-middle-class, predominantly white neighborhood. You would think that children of privilege, the local kids whose families didn't have pressure on them financially, would have had the wherewithal to be generous with their peers, particularly the ones who struggle. You'd also think that those parents would have taught their children to be kind to people with disabilities and who face extraordinary challenges. That wasn't the case.

Clearly, there's something about wealth and entitlement

that makes some people think they are exempt from the struggles of life, that they are somehow superior to others who don't have it so easy because universally, it was the bused-in kids, the kids who came from no privilege and whose families lived in poverty, who were nice and generous with Emily. They knew what it was like to struggle and they felt a kinship with Emily.

Those kids were kind to her. They wrote her sweet notes, gave her gifts, and wanted to play on the swings with her during recess and sat with her in class. These small human kindnesses added up.

Contrast that with the way Emily was treated by the kids in the neighborhood and the difference was appalling. People often measure intelligence by what you say, and when you're unable to speak, they make the automatic assumptions that you're stupid and have nothing worthwhile to add, and thus they believe they're free to treat you poorly. It's time we move beyond that limited, ignorant thinking.

The local kids, almost every one of them, made fun of Emily. Little sniggers, laughing behind a hand, fingers pointed, mocking the sounds she made, her failed attempts at speech, and her sometimes uncoordinated movements. It went on all around her, though she often didn't notice—or if she did, she pretended otherwise.

Emily attended an afterschool gymnastics program. To accommodate the tumbling, the doors to the classrooms all along the school hallway were closed so the kids could have the length of the hallway to run and do cartwheels. Emily experienced challenges with some gross motor skills and she couldn't do everything the neurotypical kids could in the gymnastics class, but she enjoyed herself.

I arrived after the class had started. I was still outside and noticed kids standing in the breezeway at the window, peering in. I had a sick feeling. I walked closer to see what had them so enthralled. I shaded my eyes with my hand to see into the hallway and blanched. They were all watching Emily, focused on her, pointing at her, ridiculing and laughing at her.

I don't know if Emily saw or noticed. I prayed that she didn't. She didn't need one more person, particularly any of her school peers, making fun of her. Still, I saw what they did and I was furious.

"Please go away," I said, trying so hard to keep a civil tongue. They were only first-grade children, I know. You would think they'd have known better, that their parents would have taught them to be more kind.

AS HER FIRST-GRADE school year in the mainstream class wound down, we received a letter from the special education director of the Los Angeles Unified School District (LAUSD). "The school your child is enrolled in is not your school of residence," the letter said, all but reprimanding us for having sought out the opportunity. The letter's intent was obvious. Emily was being asked to leave.

I TRIED TO keep my spirits up by viewing Emily's circumstance as a problem to be solved. I've always liked puzzles and games as they all involve problem-solving strategies. I sought out information that would help me with this one. I proceeded on that theory and went to every conference possible, attended seminars, lectures, impromptu meetings, parent meetings, and District meetings.

I learned of a conference sponsored by the Autism Society of Greater Long Beach and took the day off from work to attend, and for the second time in a few short years encountered the idea of facilitated communication (FC). I'd first been introduced to FC "typers" a few years earlier at the Burbank office of the Autism Society of Los Angeles. They'd been mostly older adults, and though I'd been mildly interested in the idea, it hadn't really stuck with me. Later, I watched the 2011 feature-length documentary *Wretches & Jabberers*, which follows two middle-aged men who learned to type in later life and how their life experiences opened up dramatically after acquiring that ability.

At the Long Beach conference, speech pathologist Darlene Hanson gave a presentation that focused on one of her students, Sue Rubin, a young woman of college age. Using FC, Darlene had taught Sue to communicate via typing on a small device called an AlphaSmart. The idea flitted in and out of my brain, planting the seed. Where, I wondered, did the autistic person get the language to draw from in order to type? I also attended a presentation by a woman from the Whittier school district. Her words advocating for full inclusion in neurotypical classrooms resonated with me and guided me.

"When you're included," she said, "your child is included."

I was determined that both Emily and I would be fully integrated in the next school we moved her to.

"Give them a reason to care about your child," the speaker said. I took her words to heart.

I could no longer send my child to school and trust the educational professionals to bring the same level of care and concern I would bring. I would have to get myself into her classroom, onto the campus, into the day-to-day life of the school if I wanted to be sure Emily found her way. Everyone in the new school would know my face and therefore know Emily. I would compel them to care about her.

I'd once read a book by Oliver Sacks about a child with neurological challenges he'd worked with. In describing the child, he'd written something like "I don't remember the child so much, but I do remember the mother."

I was going to be that mother.

AS I LOOKED for ways to implement that plan, we still didn't know if anything we were doing was helping Emily, but we *did* know she treasured our reading time together. Whenever we opened a book, she settled down and paid attention. She sat on the couch next to us and appeared to follow along, though we could never be sure how much she was absorbing. Maybe she just liked the sounds of our voices. Maybe the words simply flowed over her and never made contact. We didn't know.

Reading became the key activity to fill our evenings. We read to her all forms of literature—newspapers, novels, thrillers, poetry. If it was on a piece of paper, we read it, often until we were hoarse.

Through hearing words, I hoped Emily would come to understand the rhythm and syncopation of language and then spontaneously one day might begin to talk. Honestly, I had not a clue that the words she heard were being stored away in her mind-computer, just waiting to spill out when she was ready to share her thoughts.

When reading time was over and we put her to bed, though, that's when some of the worst stress gripped us. Not every night, but three nights a week on average, after we tucked her in and Tom and I got settled, her shrieking and screaming began in earnest. I believed we should let her cry it out, as parents of that era were taught to do with young children learning to sleep on their own. Tom, however, disagreed. He was worried about brain damage. In moments of upset, Emily hit herself with the heel of her hand on her upper forehead. This happened so frequently that the area along her hairline had stopped growing hair. She developed a permanent red spot there.

"When she hits herself, that's what so upsets me," Tom told me. "I was really concerned, still am, that she's damaging herself. It's pretty awful. I couldn't let her do it."

When the meltdowns occurred, Tom went into her room and placed his hand over her forehead so that when she tried to strike herself, she ended up hitting his hand instead.

I worried that this would only make her angrier. I could hear it: the more he tried to get in the middle of her self-harm, the more her screaming intensified. She was angry, and Tom's interventions only made it worse. "Cut it out, Tom!"

"I can't let her keep hurting herself," he hollered back, frustrated. Our two adult voices bellowing at each other joined with Emily's howls of outrage. The house pulsed with raised voices, each one of us indignant and at odds with the others.

Eventually, he wore Emily down and the screaming subsided. When he came back to our bedroom, my husband was bloodied from her scratching. We tended to his wounds. Short of removing her fingernails, we didn't know how to stop Emily's tendency to maul. Putting up with these nocturnal outbursts was exhausting.

It was in moments like these that Tom and I recognized we really only had each other, and we were grateful for at least that. No family members ever offered to watch her. We had no trusted employees we could pay to carry the burden for a bit. It was too much to ask of friends. All we had was the constant drumbeat of Emily's needs, which filled up the hours between work and sleep. We felt isolated from the larger community, and though we were in this together, Tom and I frequently felt adrift and alone. We weren't original in this way. Ask other parents of special needs children: you simply do what you have to do. We weren't superhuman and often felt crushed by the weight of what we carried.

WITH OUR COMMITMENT to having Emily fully included, we moved her to our local school, Encino Elementary, to have her integrated into a neurotypical class. It was second grade. She would be the first autistic student ever to be included at that school.

True to the pledge I'd made to myself at the autism conference, I was always in the classroom, helping in the school's front office, getting to know the teachers and the principal, getting people to care about Emily. I started a Girl Scout troop to ensure she was included. I was the parent volunteer in the classroom, the vice president of the PTA. Whatever it took.

With her aide, Emily participated daily in the regular academic life. I could tell she was learning to decode letters and words because she regularly brought me videotapes, wordlessly getting my attention to view them, having read the packaging to know that the subject interested her. She was also able to do some of the class arithmetic work using a method called TouchMath that Alicia had taught her. She wasn't taking the tests and doing all the regular classroom activities, but on her own terms, she was progressing academically. She was fitting in, developing friendships; she was beloved by the teachers and learning to be socially appropriate.

I liked being in the full-inclusion classes. I have always liked being around people that I could see as examples of how I wanted to be, people I could model my behavior on. I tread carefully here because I stand with my community. That said, I have always favored the company of non-autistic people. There's a different feeling entirely being around neurotypical people because they give off less random energy compared with autistic people. And they offer more predictability, something that gives me comfort. I stand with my community, but I also know this preference is there.

I must have stood out among my peers. I may not be able to speak, but I am always making random sounds. Plus, my body does things that people don't expect. When something brings me joy, for instance, it can be so intense that I am filled by fits of laughter and I may move more erratically than normally.

A lot of kids are pretty wild at that age and in some ways I fit in because of that. You would think that hearing all the chatting of the kids in the classroom would have overwhelmed me, but actually, I loved it.

Some teachers pulled my parents into a meeting when I was in Kindergarten. I remember it clearly though Mom and Dad might not. The teachers were worried about my lack of verbal skills. They began to question everything about me. Like my age, maybe I was too young. Maybe I had hearing issues. Maybe I had some kind of birth injury my parents had hidden. They had this meeting with me present. I was super young and did not really understand, it only made sense later. But I remember my parents' reaction. They looked gutted, like someone just told them I was not their child. Like all this was their fault. It made me feel so sad for them. I felt like I let them down when I thought about it years later.

I made acquaintances in school. A lot of people knew me and I knew a lot of people. But if someone approached me, they'd start to talk. It was how people made connection. The fact I didn't talk stopped me from making those strong connections. The kid who'd approached me would go away after a short time and I'd feel some relief because I couldn't join the conversation.

There was one girl who used to always come find me at recess.

"Want to go swing?" she'd ask.

Swinging was my favorite thing and I think it was hers, too. I loved that she'd come and ask me and we'd go and swing together. I was a happy child in elementary school.

There was the playground at the school that I feared at first and yet I learned to love it. The playground was always a challenge to me. Yet, I just felt happiest learning on my terms and I felt I could do that on the playground.

One day, I was with a group of kids on the playground. They had a big rubber ball and asked me right at the start of nutrition if I wanted to play kickball with them. Soon, though, they could tell I did not catch well. One of the girls began rolling the ball to me instead of kicking it and I could catch the ball that way. It worked! And I fit in.

9

"Have you ever thought about changing your practice?" The lawyer who'd represented us asked me this question out of the blue one day when Emily was in fourth grade. Up to this point, my law practice had focused on civil litigation and financial matters. Frankly, I was bored with it and tired of fighting for corporations. All I ever did was improve their bottom lines and move around decimal points for them.

"I've never thought about it." I was honest with her.

"I think you should. I'd love to have you join my practice."

Though her question was completely unexpected, it could not have come at a better time. I'd become a fierce and relentless campaigner for Emily and those skills could help other children. It was crazy, but I basically sued our school district annually from the time Emily was in preschool through high school. Once I realized what the law promised her, and how little the school district was doing to make good on those promises, I went after them tooth and nail. I had a lot of experience by this point.

"What do you think?" I asked Tom that night about the job shift.

"You'd be so great at it. You care so much about the kids. And besides, we'd finally get you down here working with the real people." He still teased me about my corporate clients. Tom himself had also shifted in his career, going on to become a court commissioner—basically a judge, adjudicating cases in Los Angeles.

WITHIN A YEAR, I shuttered my practice to join hers. In taking on that work, I came to realize the value of preschool teachers and their incredible perceptivity and astute evaluations of young children. I remembered the woman from the Magic Years and her statement that Emily didn't know what was expected of her. She was so insightful. Preschool teachers have seen so many children. They notice when the behaviors are out of the norm. Working as an advocate for parents of special needs children, I represented many families. I would always ask during our initial meeting: "When did you first know there was an issue?" I'd often get a similar answer: "I didn't notice until years later, but a preschool teacher once told me . . ." Preschool teachers tend to catch details that doctors, parents, and experts don't catch until years later.

It turns out that my experience with Emily was extremely valuable in helping these other families.

"How do you know so much about this?" clients asked me. I told them about Emily. I never held back personal details. Emily and my clients all grew up together.

I discovered I was a natural at representing these kids

and their parents. I was never any less aggressive in my advocacy for a client than I had been for Emily. I changed children's lives, as well as those of their parents and siblings. Sometimes, a small alteration, like an added service or a change of placement to a different school, can make a huge transformation in a child's life.

Recently, I received a note from a young woman.

"You may not remember me, but you helped me in middle school. You made sure I got into the class I needed and everything got better after that. It changed my life. Now I'm good. I'm graduating high school this spring and going on to college. You helped me. Thank you."

I've received scores of letters, cards, and emails just like that. Apart from raising Emily, this legal work has been the most rewarding thing I've ever done.

"WHAT DO YOU think about facilitated communication?" I asked Alicia Elliott in a conference on Emily's progress when she was about eleven and Tom and I were still looking for solutions. I remembered the woman I'd first encountered at the Long Beach autism conference, Darlene Hanson, who'd had great success getting autistic kids to type to communicate. She might be able to help. I told Alicia what I remembered about Darlene's client Sue Rubin.

"Could Emily do the same?" I asked.

Alicia shook her head. "Emily has verbal communicative intent," she said, explaining that Emily clearly wanted to make herself known and was making strides to do so. Any other form of communication—sign language, facilitated communication—might impede her progress toward speech.

"You still think that's possible, that she'll talk one day? After all this time?" I asked. I was losing hope.

"I do. We wouldn't want anything to interfere with that intent," Alicia said.

Of course we wouldn't want that. Alicia must be right. We'd trusted her every step of the way. She'd always had Emily's back. She was the expert. She must be right. If learning to type might interfere, I trusted her. I dropped my queries about FC.

AS MIDDLE SCHOOL loomed, we needed to find yet another place for our daughter. On the recommendation of Emily's fifth-grade teacher, but against the advice of all others who worked with Emily, we began considering alternative placements for middle school, including placement in a specialized academic setting known as a Non-Public School. I was worried that the bullying I had observed in elementary school would become impossible in middle school, a time notoriously challenging for all students, let alone those with special needs.

TOM TOOK IT on to see if the Non-Public School was a viable option. "This wonderful teacher introduced herself to me and went over, in incredible detail, all the ways she'd be able to work with Emily," Tom told me after attending an open house for a Non-Public School middle school, certified by the state to provide specialized educational services for students like Emily. "She was great. This is a perfect placement."

With that, the decision was made. With the support of

the district, we abandoned our local public school in favor of this specialized setting. It was the opposite of the full inclusion we'd fought so hard for, yet we were excited. The future looked good with a stalwart educator in our corner.

On the first day of sixth grade, however, when we arrived at Emily's assigned classroom, we found a different teacher, one not at all as interested in working with Emily as the one Tom had met. Emily had been reassigned to a different class and no explanation given.

"I was so angry," Tom said. "Why didn't they warn us about the change or prepare us somehow?"

Her new teacher's previous job had been as a shoe salesman. He was employed on an "emergency credential," had zero special education experience, and had never even taught school before. We hired occupational and behavioral therapists who occasionally attended class with her, and they reported regularly how badly things were going, but we didn't know where else to turn.

We sent a privately retained behaviorist to the school to take a look at how things were going. While still in the school, unable to contain how upset she was, she called. "You need to remove Emily immediately. They don't understand her and her abilities." She was crying. "The teacher gives her the same jigsaw puzzle to do over and over again. It's just wrong."

I asked the school to provide daily evidence of Emily's academic work. Every day I received promises that they'd meet my request, but they never did. The final straw came halfway through seventh grade when I went in to observe her "science" class. The teacher put on a video of the *Magic School Bus* cartoon featuring Ms. Frizzle, who imparted the so-called lesson. That was it. I pretty much carried Emily out of the classroom that day, determined to move her to our local public middle school.

"I CAN'T BELIEVE those people." I came into the house, slamming down my briefcase on the entry table. "Why do we have to put up with such incompetence?" I'd just been to yet another IEP.

Tom met me at the door. "Not good?"

"Ineptitude! Imbeciles! Cretins! Boneheads! They want to screw us out of whatever we ask for." I kicked off my shoes, railing about what I'd just faced, trying to get Emily placed as a fully included student in our local middle school. "I won't have it."

Emily was upstairs, and though likely to overhear my outburst, I didn't care. "They are nefarious know-nothings who have no business working in education. And I told them so. To their faces." My words echoed off the walls.

"Valerie . . ." Tom shook and then lowered his head. He often parroted my mom's adage: *You catch more flies with honey than vinegar.* I didn't want to catch any damn flies. I wanted my daughter educated. "We have to make nice with them. That's the only way this is going to work."

"I am *not* going to make nice, Tom. We don't have time for this crap. They're not being nice in denying Emily what she needs." I was fed up.

Tom and I are different people and we have very different styles when it comes to working with others, differences that were exacerbated when dealing with school administrators. Tom is a team player, a negotiator. He's really good at working with people and convincing them he likes them, even if he doesn't.

Early in our marriage, we attended a party together. A deputy district attorney, whom I knew he vehemently disliked, was there. Yet I saw him go up to her, chat with her, laugh with her, and then—I couldn't believe it—he actually hugged her. He was a defense attorney. She was a prosecutor. They were basically enemies.

"I thought you told me she was a bitch?" I whispered to him when he came back to my side of the room.

"Oh, she is." He laughed. "But I have to make nice. That's how this whole thing works."

I, on the other hand, have never once in my life been able to be anything but transparent in how I feel. If I dislike someone, trust me, they'll know it. I have absolutely no ability to hide my feelings. That candidness, alas, did not earn me many friends in dealing with the Los Angeles Unified School District.

These were difficult years, and I'm still astonished that we survived them. We were dealing with not just Emily and her limitations and behavioral issues—the nighttime screaming and hitting and scratching, which would tire out even the most saintly parent—but having to fight the school system on a regular basis on top of it. Not only did I have to sue the school district repeatedly to get her the services to which we she was legally entitled, but I was hated and reviled by administrators, teachers, school district personnel across the board for doing so.

Every time I went to an IEP meeting, I was met with a roomful of people who clearly scorned me. Mostly I was the one who had to attend these meetings and reported back to

Tom. Each time I had to face off with a handful of professionals who just wanted me to go away. In no time, I saw that they were all out to do as little as they could for Emily; they had bad intentions. That sounds harsh, but it was true. Their job was to save the school district as much money as possible. Mine was to get my daughter's needs met. We battled.

Each time, before I walked into the conference room for an IEP meeting, I had to put on my imaginary armor to deal with the eye-rolling, the scoffing, the shaking heads, the dismissive glances. After the meeting, I'd tell Tom what had transpired. He was always interested and supportive, but he wasn't in the room with me, he wasn't the one having to don the armor. He didn't see the faces they made at me. He couldn't defend or protect me from what was happening in the way he wanted to. It created a resentment I didn't want to feel. I felt like I was overly burdened—caring for Emily, fighting for her rights with the school district, managing a household, practicing law, pursuing a social life, and maintaining my relationship with my husband. Some days, it was just too much.

I FINALLY SUCCEEDED in moving her back to the local public school. There, I met a science teacher who saw potential in Emily. "I think she should be in honors science," he said. "It would be a calmer environment for her, and she would do better there than with the kids in the regular class."

We were thrilled and whole-heartedly agreed. The principal, however, was opposed.

"As a special education student, Emily is ineligible for honors classes." He refused to move her, even though the teacher had requested it. Whenever we questioned these kinds of decisions, that principal gave the same refrain in a sarcastic voice.

"You know what's so special about this student? Her *parents* are what's so special." He, a professional educator, a principal, derided us for advocating for our child.

I later had to write a cease-and-desist letter to this principal, who'd decided he'd videotape Emily in class to demonstrate that she had no business attending general education classes. My language in that letter was harsh. That's what it took, and how nasty things got, over and over again.

EMILY GREW AND adolescence became an issue. I couldn't always tell how much she understood about anything I told her, so I didn't go into a long, detailed explanation of menstruation to prepare her. I just kept my eyes peeled for signs that I'd need to address it. One day, I was preparing the laundry when I saw blood on her panties.

"Emily, honey." I took her into the bathroom and showed her a box of sanitary pads. "You're having a period." I had her remove her stained underwear and handed her a fresh pair. "This happens to all women; it's nothing to be alarmed by. You will need to use a pad when this happens." I showed her how to use it. She wasn't bothered in the slightest. In no time, though, Tom and I noticed the hormonal shifts. On the days leading up to her period, what I had previously thought was impossible happened: the meltdowns got even worse, the screaming louder, the upset greater.

I'd always had wicked PMS, and now the same hormones were wreaking havoc in Emily. Even Tom got into the act. "I started to feel like I was having PMS, too," he said. "It was all too much."

I talked with a gynecologist who suggested birth control pills to regulate her cycle and even out the hormonal roller coaster. Emily took a dose that gave her a three-month respite between periods. When we moved into the pink pills in the pack, I watched out because her period would start soon.

That said, throughout this time we tried to transfer personal agency to Emily. We communicated with her regularly that she had the power to shape her world, to control it, to be the one setting the agenda rather than us.

We enrolled her in a technology-oriented charter school for ninth and tenth grades, but it did not go well. As the academic load grew heavier, students dropped out to go to other schools. We were hoping to stay put, tired of moving her about, until an incident on Valentine's Day when she was in tenth grade changed everything.

I had just dropped Emily off and was watching to be sure she entered the school when I noticed a boy standing at the entrance to the school with a big basket of roses. As each girl approached the campus, he kind of bowed and offered her a rose. A sweet gesture for Valentine's Day, right?

When Emily approached, he extended a rose. Lovely. That would make her day.

Just as Emily reached out to receive the flower, he snatched it back and laughed at her. I could see her face, the upset, the confusion, the sting of that moment. I wanted to jump out of the car, confront that young man and call him a jerk, report him to the principal, and scream my head off at him. I would have yanked the flower from his hand and given it to her. I didn't do any of that. I didn't want to call any more attention to the moment. It was just so obvious, though: the hurt, the bewilderment. It was so painful to watch. She walked away with her shoulders dropped, her head low. I felt sickened and sat in my car crying.

From her recent writings, it's clear Emily felt relatively accepted and well treated in school, which is at odds with my recollection of those years. Yes, there were a handful of friends and acquaintances who showed her kindness, but many of the young people I witnessed didn't. They were callous and uncaring. So, either Emily didn't notice the transgressions I did—she tends to pay closer attention to what people say more than their actions—or she simply chose to set aside those cruelties. Either way, there's a lot for me to learn in how she handled those moments.

At that time, I wondered if she could handle Birmingham High School, our local district high school that served three thousand students. It might be a less competitive and stressful environment. I didn't know if she could manage herself and the social dynamics there. We were about to find out.

IN THE PROCESS of attending the IEP team meeting necessary to make that change and ensure that the services Emily had been given at the tech charter school continued at Birmingham, it became clear the district did not support keeping Emily in general education classes. After Emily had spent years as a fully included student, they were now proposing a rollback to a special day class, the same sort of class we'd fled ten years prior, one that would again isolate her from her neurotypical peers. I tried to keep my voice down in the IEP meeting, but failed miserably.

"She's already proven she can do the work and not interfere with the regular classroom." I tried not to rail, tried to channel my inner Tom, but after every IEP meeting, I wanted to head to the nearest Mexican restaurant and order a pitcher of margaritas.

Eventually, we got her fully included at Birmingham.

AFTER TORTUROUS YEARS in middle school and the first few years of high school, miraculously, her transition to Birmingham turned out to be what was needed. In no time, she was successful in her classes, and success there begat success across campus. She developed a group of girls she'd sit with during lunch, the Lunch Bunch. These girls all took to her. When they heard it was her birthday, they surprised her with a cake and goodies. Emily was in heaven; she felt welcomed and glad to be in school. She took art classes, and even had a job delivering summonses from the nurse's office. One of the service clubs that only invited kids with the highest GPA asked her to join unofficially. She didn't qualify based on her academic grades, still, the club made space for her. She was featured in the yearbook picture with the other members and was given a club sweatshirt. She couldn't do everything the others in the club did, but she did help out at events, cutting up fruit or whatever needed to be done. By the end of her time at Birmingham, she'd received academic awards. Even after a tough start with a choir teacher, who had no patience for her in his class, another music teacher welcomed her. And so it went.

IT'S IMPORTANT TO realize that kids like Emily are developmentally delayed in every way possible. While her classmates were all fully ensconced in the throes of adolescence, she was a number of steps behind them. Her brain might have been able to do things that her peers were doing, and her body was keeping up with ovulation and other milestones of maturation, but behaviorally and socially, she was nowhere near where they were. Kids in high school are making choices about having sex, or smoking pot, or drinking and driving, and they're all enjoying a new level of independence. Emily was not grappling with the same decisions, hadn't matured to make those choices, and was still quite dependent on us and her aides. If I didn't point out to her that she was having a period, for example, she might not notice. There was always a gap between her and her classmates beyond her inability to speak. When events like dances and proms came onto the scene, we were heading into dicey territory.

"MY SON WOULD be very, very happy to take Emily to prom," the mother of one of Emily's friends said in her junior year. The woman's son was a high-functioning Asperger's kid who'd invited Emily over to his house a few times.

"Are you sure? Maybe your son's already been invited to the dance." The boy had never shown that kind of interest in Emily. Emily would be fine staying home on prom night, or Tom would take her.

"No, no," the mother insisted. "We'll take her," she said, then corrected herself. "*He'll* take her. It'll be wonderful."

I worried this plan was something the mother had cooked up on her own, but she kept insisting. When I told Emily, she was excited. Most high schoolers want to be asked to the prom.

Emily had her hair, makeup, and nails done. We bought

a new dress and shoes. I ordered a boutonniere for the young man and planned to drive the two of them to the dance, along with an aide to be with Emily for the duration, in the shadows, to assist if needed.

As the night of the prom got closer, I relaxed. It would all be great. She'd have a wonderful time. I didn't need to be so overly worried.

"How'd it go?" I asked the aide when Tom and I retrieved them at the end of the night. She curtly shook her head at me. The boy, meanwhile, got into the car without saying a word. The next day the aide told us what had happened.

"It wasn't good. Emily tried not to let it get to her," the aide said, "but it was hard." When they got to the prom, the boy didn't want to dance with Emily. He didn't sit with her, or try to interact with her. Tom and I heard he'd had social struggles due to his Asperger's and had recently found himself invited into the "in" group at school. Now, apparently, having Emily at his side threatened to torpedo his social rise. "He did everything he could to distance himself from her, and when it came time to take photos together, he flat-out refused," the aide said.

The photographer quickly realized what was going on, according to the aide, and got angry with the boy, trying to persuade him to be more thoughtful and decent. All to no avail. The photographer took a picture of the boy on his own, and then one of Emily on her own.

It sickened me. I wished the mother had never put her son up to that. Emily would have been happy to go with Tom or wouldn't have cared if she'd missed it. She did not need the experience or deserve the humiliation.

A few weeks later, the prepaid prom photo came in the

mail. Emily and this young man were pictured together. How was that possible? He'd refused to be photographed with her. Then I figured it out: the photographer must have felt badly about what had happened and photoshopped it.

It was such a wonderful act of kindness, and I was touched by his gesture. Still, I put the photo away, under a pile of bills.

Prom night was a small setback, as Emily thrived in her large suburban public high school. Students knew her and liked her. Tom and I attended back-to-school nights, and as we walked the campus with Emily other students yelled out, greeting her by name. A group of neurotypical girls from her dance class liked her and invited her to do things with them occasionally. At Christmastime, they invited Emily to the mall on a shopping outing.

I was so grateful I bought the girls, Emily included, long-sleeve holiday T-shirts with reindeer on them. They all looked so cute in the shirts and Emily could not have been more pleased to be part of the group. I forgot all about that excursion, other than to hold on to the girls' kindness.

Ten years later, I was speaking to a group of behavioral aides who'd just been trained to work with students like Emily, about three hundred of them. I talked about the value of inclusion in high school, how important it had been to Emily to be with neurotypical kids, how much it mattered to her. After the talk, one of the young aides-in-training came up to me.

"Is the Emily you're talking about the one who went to Birmingham High?" she asked.

"Yes."

"I'm one of the girls who took Emily to the mall over

Christmas break. You gave us these T-shirts with deer on them," she said to jog my memory. "The whole reason I'm in this field now is because of Emily."

It was Emily who'd inspired her, she told me. She'd seen Emily in her academic classes, in her dance class, and had noticed her with an aide. Observing what Emily was capable of doing with her aide's help had changed this young woman's life. She was now looking forward to providing another young person with the kind of access Emily had experienced, and eventually becoming a speech therapist.

"If I hadn't met Emily," she said, "if she'd been kept sequestered in a special needs classroom, my career path would never have become apparent. It was all because of Emily."

The thing I have to keep in mind when I remember the sometimes-painful moments from her past is how instrumental Emily has always been in touching the lives of others. No, she didn't have close, intimate conversations with her peers in high school, she didn't have BFFs, she didn't go to prom in a frame-the-moment kind of way. She was always one step removed from the typical adolescent experience. We'd walk down the school hall, though, or run into kids outside of the campus, and they'd say hi to Emily and acknowledge her. She gathered a wide-ranging group of people around her, and was known by just about everyone in that high school with some three thousand students. Her presence had an impact. By the time her years at Birmingham ended, it was a high point for all of us.

When I was about 13 Mom said it time for me to start being responsible for myself when I was out in the world. That meant I needed to start carrying a purse. Mom picked it out for me— she's the shopper in the family, though she always makes sure

I approve, of course. The purse was gray with a long shoulder strap, nothing fancy but practical. She taught me to carry my wallet and keys, a cell phone, my ID, as well as feminine hygiene products. I also learned how to use a credit card.

At first, I found it a nuisance to carry the purse but she was insistent. She also taught me how to use the alarm system in the house—an intimidating thing—but it gave me control and independence. These were responsibilities I could have allowed others to do for me, but I needed to learn to do them for myself. Once I understood the reason for these things, I was motivated and would learn.

By the time high school rolled around, I knew it was the age when many make friends and have a group to hang out and chat with. I missed out on a lot of that. Still, I knew people and interacted with them. I had an aide with me who encouraged me to interact more than I did but I was really intimidated by the conversation aspect. I get that she wanted to push me, but in my mind I was there for school and tried to stay focused on the academic aspects rather than the social ones. I was acquainted with many kids, though.

There was a boy, one who listened to music with headphones. He'd give me one earbud and I'd listen with one ear and he'd listen with the other. I think it was like pop music—not my stuff, I prefer classical music—but I liked the experience we shared. That was nice.

At school there was another very nice boy and he was not autistic. He would always make a point of greeting me. He never lingered too long, which was good because it might have made me self-conscious. We both knew I couldn't have a long chat or anything, but he called me "Miss Emily" and I can say that it made me feel seen and noticed outside of my autism.

I do think there's a lot of judgment about nonverbal people and that others make assumptions about us. I realize that most people just don't know any better. They don't think you're intelligent and that you have nothing to say.

When I was in high school, I didn't know for sure that I'd ever be able to really communicate with others, though I had a picture of being able to do so in my mind. I had the belief that it could happen, though. I always had the belief.

The big thing that kept me apart, though, was that I didn't have a clear path out of adolescence like most of the others. They could assume that they'd move out of the family house one day, have boyfriends, go to college, or whatever. Those are such normal things that I knew would not happen normally for me. I didn't know what would happen with me. As I got older, I started to feel more urgency around that. "What the hell am I going to do when Mom can't speak for me?!" That started to become a worry.

10

EVOKING PLACE

Maybe I'm where I should be but who knows.
Maybe no one here has a goddamn clue
Maybe this will be the end of the stale me.
Maybe this will lift me out of the muck
Maybe people really are what they say
Who knows, maybe people don't listen well
I'll say it louder without using voice
Become the crowd itself, a walking herd
Maybe it's just a desk inside a room
Maybe it's where I learn to be me

"I'm signing up immediately. It sounds perfect for my son."

"Me, too. The facilities there are marvelous—have you been? It's right by the beach. With all the interaction they'll have with each other, they'll barely notice we're not there. It'll be great. The perfect option."

The word flying around among the group of parents we'd bonded with at Valley Beth Shalom, all of whom were raising special needs young adults, was that a new facility opening in Laguna Beach was the promised land. Everyone was excited, falling over each other to sign their kids up.

"That's pretty far away," Tom said. "Seventy-five miles. What is that, about three hours if traffic is bad?"

"Still, it might be nice for her," I suggested.

"You know, a lot of neurotypical kids are still not ready to be on their own immediately after high school. Sometimes they need a year or two at home, attending community college, before they're ready to venture out. If neurotypical kids aren't ready for this step, aren't we asking too much of Emily?"

"But maybe Emily's ready," I ventured.

"She just graduated high school. Isn't this a bit soon?"

We decided we should check it out. To be honest, by this point we were looking for a break for us as much as we wanted progress for Emily. Tom and I were worn down. Once high school had ended, all regular activities for Emily came to a halt, except the ones we set up for her. Meanwhile, her screaming at night and sometimes during the days was increasing. We were often bloodied by her scratching, looking like human pincushions. The fact that she'd grown into an adult body with full adult strength didn't help. We needed a plan to keep her occupied.

ON A DAY in midsummer, Tom, Emily, and I made the trek to Laguna Beach, a small coastal artist community in Orange County known for its surf spots, art festivals, galleries, marine sanctuaries, and hiking trails with fabulous ocean views.

"What do you think, Emily? Would you like to try living here?" I didn't know how much she understood, but she was willing.

The rooms in this converted motel, now designed as a residential care facility for young adults with developmental disabilities, all faced the Pacific Ocean. Staff members, we were told, would help the residents develop self-care routines, learn how to plan their own meals and grocery shop, practice managing their money, and learn housekeeping skills. A common room for playing games and hanging out together beckoned, promising bonding and friendship. There was so much to like. That the facility was located within the cozy Laguna Beach community gave us hope that our young adults would be incorporated into the small-town life and feel as if they belonged—unlikely in the expanse of LA, where someone like Emily might easily get lost in the hustle.

I spoke with the staff and explained Emily's situation. "She has behavioral issues."

"No worries. We can handle it."

"She's pretty well nonverbal."

"That's okay. We got it."

The enthusiasm among our group of parents grew to a febrile pitch. The place would open in August. "You better get her signed up, if you want in. It'll be full before you know it."

The only other option on the table was Pathway at UCLA Extension, but they'd already denied her entrance as a live-in student due to her language limitations and behavioral issues. Pathway said we could enroll her in the program as a commuter student, since they weren't equipped to deal with the behaviors and lack of language on a live-in basis.

This beach-living option was the better choice. Still, it

was hard to envision her living so far away from us. How would she manage so many of the day-to-day challenges Tom and I were used to mediating?

"What do you think, Emily? Do you want to try this?"

"Yes."

WE PICKED OUT a room for her on the first floor, nearest the hub of activity—we didn't want her on one of the upper floors where she would be more isolated—and then started to buy things. This must be what it's like to be the parent of a college-bound student. Endless trips to Bed Bath & Beyond, Target, and the Container Store followed as we stockpiled lamps and bedding, towels and toiletries, even a carrier to hold the toiletries. A laundry basket, a shower curtain, a chair for the room, art for the walls. Our family room started to look like a warehouse. We gathered enough stuff that we needed to hire a van to transport it all.

The day the facility opened, we made the drive south to move Emily in. All the others were moving in that day as well. People bustled about, unloading cars and trucks, carrying chairs and linens and furniture. Staff members yelled over the melee; it was absolute chaos.

Emily did a good job holding herself together as we spent hours arranging her room.

"Em, I have a special gift for you." I offered her a small gift-wrapped box. "To commemorate this day."

Excitedly, she tore the paper and pulled out the handmade necklace I'd ordered. Made from a flattened silver spoon, and adorned with crystal flowers, the pendant necklace hung on a long silver chain. Her name, as well as my name and phone number, were inscribed on the back, just in case.

When our efforts were done, the room was gorgeous; all of our preparations had paid off. We looked out her window at the peaceful view of the Pacific. Other parents and young adults stopped by to see the decor.

"Love those lamps."

"What a fabulous room. Congrats, Emily."

"Such an exciting day."

The staff showed us all the things she could do at Glennwood House: play cards or board games, do art, or put together puzzles.

She was bewildered. There were just so many people and so much to take in. Of course she was bewildered.

Within hours of our arrival, the staff developed suspicions about Emily, concerns that she wasn't going to fit in, that this wasn't going to work. They watched us incessantly. As the day wore on and started to take a toll on Emily, she got aggressive, mostly with Tom. She hugged him and dug into him with her nails, hurting him.

"Thanks for the nice hug, Emily." He tried to downplay it, breaking off the embrace, but one of the women on staff saw. She shook her head in disapproval.

The facility had been promoted as a place that could handle kids who were autistic and nonverbal, but most of the other residents were young adults with Down syndrome. Almost all of them had cognitive limitations. I wasn't sure if it was a good fit. Meanwhile, that staff member kept giving us the side-eye.

WE GOT EMILY'S room settled, her clothes put away, her necklace on. She had dinner with the group and now needed some alone time.

"Okay, Emily. We're taking off. We'll see you in the morning."

We hugged and kissed her goodbye, leaving her in her new room, then headed to a hotel.

If we had it to do over again, I think we could have made it work. The smart thing would have been to rent an apartment for myself nearby for about a month to ease Emily into this situation. At the time, though, we had not thought it through.

THE NEXT MORNING we returned ready to congratulate her on this move toward independence, all set to high-five her on this step into adulthood. When we entered the facility the smell of pancakes and scrambled eggs filled the space as the staff cleaned dishes from the recent breakfast. I hoped she'd had a good breakfast. She loved pancakes.

When we got to her room, we were startled. Emily was standing there, still in her nightgown, dazed and befuddled. The lamps that had been so admired by visitors yesterday were knocked over, one broken. Everything in the perfectly appointed room was now askew. The necklace I'd had made for her was broken into bits. Breakfast had come and gone and no one had come to check on her, to invite her to breakfast, to make sure that she ate.

Every light fixture in her room was lit, the bulbs hot. They'd been on all night. Likely, she'd tried to figure out how to turn them off and knocked them over in her attempts. She may have broken the necklace when she couldn't figure out how to take it off to go to bed and no one had come to help her. She was visibly exhausted and distressed.

Best as I could figure out, she'd been awake the entire night, likely standing there the whole time confused and disoriented. It was like the bar mitzvah when she'd been an infant, left standing in her crib, alone and upset.

My heart broke. What had we done to her? I took her in my arms and tried to comfort her, though she didn't want my hugs. I tried to look her in the eye but she averted her gaze.

"Do you want to go home?" I asked.

"Yes."

I wasn't sure if I wanted to break down and cry or rage at the staff, only that I was so upset and needed to protect my child, whom they'd taken in with no real ability to care for her. We started to pack up the room we'd only arranged some eighteen hours earlier.

"What are you doing?" A facility staffer passed me as I was carrying a chair back to our rented van. He was perplexed.

"We're leaving. Moving Emily back home."

"Why?"

"I was told this was a place equipped to serve the needs of nonverbal autistic individuals," I said, trying to keep my tone civil, trying not to blow up. "That's clearly not the case."

"Whoever told you that?" he replied. Rather than make excuses, he off-loaded the blame onto me, implying somehow that *I* was the one who had misunderstood. I could not even respond.

I'd had countless discussions with the staff prior to this move. We'd explained Emily's challenges over and over. I'd been assured repeatedly they could address her needs. Clearly, they could not.

After all that effort, she was a mess and we were done.

Many of the items we'd so lovingly selected for her room

I gave away to the other residents. Items still in their packaging that could be returned, we took back with us. We bundled our daughter and those few things into the van and made our way back to safety, back to home.

"LOOK, CAN WE do this?" I got on the phone the following Monday morning. "I know it's late and the school year is starting. We thought we had something else in place, but now UCLA looks like the best bet. Can we make it work?"

I'd previously been in touch with the UCLA Pathway program, but had not yet spoken with the Regional Center,* the California agency that provided support to the students attending the UCLA program. Now I needed both of them on board to make this work. First UCLA agreed. Thank goodness. We needed a plan in place for Emily. Having her home full-time, with us as the only source of entertainment or distraction, was not going to work.

I called the Regional Center next. "She needs one-on-one support for Pathway, immediately. Can you help?"

They could. It was like a miracle, how quickly it all came together. If she needed to be a commuter student to attend at UCLA, so be it. We'd make it work.

PATHWAY IS A two-year transitional program for students with intellectual and other developmental disabilities that

---

* Regional Centers are private, nonprofit corporations that contract with the California Department of Developmental Services to provide and/ or coordinate services and supports for individuals with developmental disabilities.

provides educational, social, and vocational experiences. The program was promoted as having a really big bonus: Pathway students could attend classes and participate with UCLA students in the social, recreational, and cultural life of a major university. Emily would be with other stimulating, learning young people—at least some of the time. That was a huge draw. She was bright and she thrived when surrounded by others of similar intellectual abilities. This would be better for her.

EMILY COMPLETED THE first year as a commuter student, and received services from an agency which provided community-based and supported living services for individuals on the autism spectrum. Steven and his associate Cassandra worked for that agency. Steven had learned the ropes of the business from having been an aide himself. We'd developed a friendship with him, and he often came to our house to visit.

"I know you wanted Emily to live on campus," he told us one day during a visit. "I've been thinking of launching my own company with Cassandra. Emily could be our start-up client. We could arrange to provide her with twenty-four/seven support so she could live on her own at UCLA."

"You know it's more than just the daily living skills?" I asked. "The behaviors can be an issue, as well as her not talking."

"I get it. We've worked a lot with her."

"Would you want to take this on? It's a big job."

"I promise you, we'll pull out all the stops for Emily. We can make this work."

After Steven left, Tom and I talked it over. It had been a year and a half since the Glennwood debacle. We were not even sure we wanted her to continue at Pathway as the program had not delivered as promised. The inclusion with the UCLA students never really panned out. We still wanted Emily to have a life that provided inclusion in her community.

Now, with Steven's commitment and his understanding of what we sought for Emily, this might be possible. Together with Steven, we developed a plan for her to live on campus for year two.

WE SIGNED A lease for a one-bedroom apartment next to the campus, then headed to CORT to rent furniture. We picked out a couch to go in the living room with a fold-out bed for the aide who would be hired to stay overnight with Emily, making sure it was as high-end as possible. We didn't want the aide to be uncomfortable. We also selected all the essentials: bed, dining set, a television.

Soon, the apartment was decked out and we had a plan with Steven and Cassandra for round-the-clock care, funded by the Regional Center. The staff helped Emily with day-to-day skills like cooking, showering, and cleaning her apartment, and they brought her to and from the UCLA Pathway classes and extracurricular activities.

When she first moved into the apartment, it was an adjustment. After a while, though, Tom and I started to enjoy the freedom. We could go out for dinner on the spur of the moment, plan a weekend away, have a drink if we felt like it, enjoy a little time for ourselves. We worked to reconnect with each other after more than two decades of focusing on Emily.

Meanwhile, Emily was blossoming. She came home on Sundays to do her laundry and to have dinner with us, but the rest of the time, we could do what we wanted. What a relief.

THE CALLS STARTED coming soon thereafter.

"Emily's aide for tonight came down with the flu and we have no one else. You'll have to stay with her."

"We're having an incident at Whole Foods. A meltdown. I need you to come right away."

"The aide scheduled for tomorrow just quit. If you want her to attend classes at Pathway, you'll need to bring her."

Cassandra or Steven called regularly, despite the fact their agency was obligated to provide her full-time care. Once, when we were in the car on our way home from the airport after a weekend trip away, her aide called. "The guy next door has been hearing all the screaming. He wants to call the police."

"No! Don't do that. Tell him we're coming right now. We'll set it right."

I calmed Emily while Tom went to see the young man next door, explaining that Emily was autistic and that calling the police would only exacerbate things. "He was only like twenty years old," Tom said. "A college kid. I don't think he fully understood, but he agreed to not call in the authorities."

We wanted to see how she'd manage in the world without us, but we kept getting tugged back in. I got frustrated.

"This is ridiculous," I told Tom. "It's their job to be sure she has staff coverage. God knows they're being paid enough." I never should have trusted Steven.

"MAYBE YOU SHOULD take her to a movie or something to make up for the fact that the soccer game's not going to happen," I mentioned to Emily's aide Marcia after a planned outing had been abruptly canceled due to weather. Emily had been looking forward to the outing, and when changes happened and she wasn't fully aware of what was going on, it could set her off.

A few hours later, Steven was on the phone. "Okay, Valerie. Enough is enough. Marcia did what you suggested and Emily got totally out of hand when she realized they weren't going to soccer. She screamed and got aggressive. Now Marcia refuses to work for her and I don't know what to do about this."

"You *said* you could handle her."

"I need you to arrange behavioral therapy. This is too much."

"What Emily needs is for someone to tell her clearly what's going on and why."

"We do that already. It doesn't fix it. It's her behaviors that need to change."

Tom was also focused on the behavioral issues. "Her meltdowns were my concern," he said later. "We needed to rein them in. Valerie was looking ahead more than I was. She understood the communication issue and the frustration it was causing Emily in a way I didn't."

Despite my knowing on some level that her acting out was tied to her inability to communicate, we arranged for

134

additional behavior modification therapy. When Emily was armed with a solid rationale, she was completely reasonable. I'd seen it. When things happened and she didn't know what was happening, that's when she got upset—understandably. I would, too.

Unlike me, she couldn't say to those around her, "Please explain it to me. I don't understand."

11

The night Cassandra called to tell us the police were at Emily's UCLA apartment was in January 2016, effectively ending Emily's experience with supported living. The agency Steven and Cassandra had formed with Emily as their foundation client was pretty much done with us. Emily had become more trouble to them than she was worth. By the time we got the call, we felt we were battling both the agency and the autism.

I reported the incident to Emily's psychiatrist, Dr. Wolf.

"Well, that's just so typical of these situations. The aides, the agencies—they're not listening to who these people are. They're the ones who allowed this situation to escalate." We felt similarly, but didn't know what to do about it. We paid out the lease on her apartment, let the Regional Center know what had occurred, had the rental furniture picked up, and that was that. We were back to square one.

"WOMAN WITH ASPERGER'S shot, killed by police in Arizona" read a link to a news story on my computer screen. My heart thundered.

It was two weeks after the UCLA debacle and I was in

my office replying to emails. That Tom and I had made the decision to remove Emily from the UCLA apartment and move her home with us felt like admitting failure. Emily appeared defeated as well. We hired Marta Amaya to assist her during the workday and we resumed caring for her during the overnight hours and weekends, as we had throughout most of her life.

This news link, though, slammed me. I read the article and learned that a twenty-four-year-old woman had been shot and killed by Phoenix-area police after a concerned friend alerted police that the woman might be suicidal. The victim had previously made a popular YouTube video showing how her service rottweiler provided comfort to her and interrupted her self-harm when she suffered an Asperger's-related meltdown. The woman had reportedly brandished a knife she'd intended to use on herself. Now she was dead.

In that moment, everything we'd been struggling with for years came into focus. I realized that if Emily didn't learn to communicate and soon, she was next in line to be shot. Countless times Tom and I had been called to intervene when she'd had a screaming or scratching incident with her caregivers at Ralph's grocery store, at Trader Joe's, at Target, times when she'd needed to be restrained and controlled. If we hadn't been able to intervene during those incidents, the police would have been called. And then . . .

I started to hyperventilate.

The girl in the news story had been known to the police. Emily wasn't. There was nothing to keep her from ending up on the wrong end of their guns.

When I showed Tom the news article that night, he was also upset. Because he'd been a criminal defense lawyer all his career, he was hyperaware of incidents when the police overreacted. "I knew firsthand all the awful things that could happen," he said. "It terrified me."

Behaviorists were always looking for the antecedent for a given incident: What set the person off? What triggered the meltdown? Once in a while we could identify an antecedent—Emily didn't get a cookie she wanted and thus, had a fit. More often than not, though, there had been no antecedent. I now saw the situation clearly for the first time. It wasn't about the stupid cookie. There were no clear antecedents for Emily's meltdowns because they all expressed her frustration with her inability to communicate. She couldn't tell us what was wrong, and *that's* what was wrong. *That* was the antecedent. If we didn't find a way to help her release that exasperation and communicate with us, she was going to end up in serious, perhaps lethal, trouble.

I Googled the subject and read about a fifteen-year-old boy with Asperger's syndrome who'd been shot and killed by police; he'd been holding a steak knife.

One study showed that a third to a half of all police violence incidents recorded between 2013 and 2015 involved a person with some form of disability. A young man with Down syndrome was killed by police officers in Maryland after he'd attempted to go back into a movie theater without buying another ticket. Early media coverage implied that his disability was to blame for the incident and that it was a "tragic accident." In a separate example, an autistic man in Virginia was tasered and arrested after a police officer confronted him while he was sitting outside a library.

If Emily were to have a similar confrontation with police or authorities, with no language, erratic mannerisms, and sometimes aggressive behavior, she could end up the same way. I couldn't save her from everything. Still, we had to do something.

We'd already tried everything we could think of. We'd tracked down and used every behavioral, speech, social, psychiatric, occupational, and language therapy on the planet, some repeatedly. We'd consulted dozens of specialists around the country, chased down every internet lead, even the woo-woo suggestions. We'd spent a fortune on therapies and approaches to help her. To no avail. The situation was becoming more dire. Something had to change. Her communication skills had to improve, and we had to make that happen now.

"I REALLY NEED her to communicate," I explained to Deborah Budding, the neuropsychologist I'd come to know and who later helped me understand autism better.* I'd run into Deborah at a conference sponsored by Darlene Hanson, the woman I'd met years earlier with her autistic typing client Sue Rubin. I'd attended the conference because my interest in facilitated communication was reemerging. FC might be a path for Emily, though Alicia Elliott had discouraged me.

Under the harsh glow of the fluorescent lights of the conference center, I unloaded on Deborah, telling her about what was going on with Emily, the UCLA incident, the police killing the young woman in Phoenix, my fears.

"What should I do?"

"I would call Peggy Shaeffer," Deborah advised. "She's doing all this work with movement and balance, core strength, the foundations that Emily will need to be able to communicate via typing. I'd go there first."

So I did, driving Emily all the way down to Long Beach,

* https://www.ted.com/talks/daniel_wolpert_the_real_reason_for_brains/transcript?language=en

forty miles away, once a week. Peggy provided physical therapy–type work on Emily's balance and posture, having her sit on a big sphere, throwing a ball—activities meant to focus on her core and somehow prepare her to communicate. I wanted her to get closer to using a keyboard, to being ready physically to communicate in that manner, but this felt like a convoluted way to get there.

"When do you think Emily will finally be ready to try FC?" I asked Peggy after many months of therapy. I was getting frustrated. "Are we making any progress at all?"

"Oh, she won't be ready for a really long time," Peggy said.

I didn't find that answer acceptable. I called Darlene Hanson, the FC expert, directly. There was no harm in trying. By this time, I had come to know Darlene professionally through my law practice.

"Your office is too far away for us," I explained. "I was hoping there'd be someone in our area who could work with Emily."

"Actually, I have a wonderful young woman who's out on maternity leave now, but she'll be back next month," Darlene said. "She'd be a great fit for Emily. Her name is Lindsey Goodrich. Should I arrange it?"

"Yes, please. We need to do something."

THE NEXT MONTH, March 2016, Lindsey, a young woman in her early thirties, stood at our doorway. She was about five foot eight, with reddish brown hair and an infectious smile.

My shoulders dropped almost immediately. There was something comforting and knowledgeable about her that I picked up on right away.

"Emily, come here. I want you to meet someone."

Within minutes, the two young women, nearly the same age, were settled on the couch like long-lost friends.

Still, Lindsey had a job to do. She was there to see if Emily might learn to communicate via FC. In doing so, she was very kind to Emily but also rather direct.

"CAN YOU POINT to the letter 'R'?" Lindsey asked, holding up a laminated letter board, like a blown-up keyboard, and then waited to see if Emily would cooperate. "We're going to spell out some words. Let's start with 'red.'"

The idea was that if Emily could start "typing" out words on this blown-up keyboard, Lindsey could record the words and eventually, instead of just typing what Lindsey specifically asked her to type, Emily might start typing information about her experience of the world. She might start genuinely communicating with us.

However, no matter what Lindsey tried, Emily wasn't interested in typing with her, though she did enjoy Lindsey's visits. Lindsey tried different approaches—using a computer keyboard, pointing at pictures, asking Emily to finish sentences. Emily responded somewhat, but we could see that nothing was clicking.

I was still hopeful. I'm doggedly optimistic, sometimes to a fault, but that optimism wasn't formidable enough to see me through the coming days.

DARLENE HANSON, LINDSEY'S supervisor, came to observe a session, to assess what was happening and make recommendations. After watching and interacting with Emily for a bit, I asked Darlene what she thought. "Will Emily ever learn to type?"

"I don't think so. My experience is that FC works best with those who have virtually no language at all. Emily can say her name and a few words. She already has too much language," she said. "I'm sorry."

Too much language? She had almost no language. I was devastated. Emily couldn't say more than a handful of words verbally and many of them were so garbled as to be unintelligible. It was hard to accept that answer. There was nothing else left.

"Don't give up hope," Darlene said, sensing my distress. "Lindsey is trained in speech therapy as well. I'll have her work on articulation practice with Emily to see if we can get her speech to come across clearer." It was a poor solution, but the only one we had.

OVER THE NEXT five months, Lindsey came to the house weekly for one hour. Together they read stories. Lindsey asked Emily questions about the stories to see if and how she might answer, verbally or on a keyboard—usually she didn't.

My aide at UCLA didn't get me. That was the problem.

It was the end of the day. I was very tired and she began writing on the whiteboard what I would be doing the next day. What she wrote was either wrong, or the plans had changed— it's a little blurry now, trying to remember. I tried to express that I didn't agree with what she was writing, but she didn't stop. Really, she just ignored me.

My experience with other caregivers had been different.

Even if I couldn't explain what, exactly, was wrong, they'd stop writing on the board and talk to me about what had changed. Or, seeing that I was upset, would leave it alone until we could come to some understanding.

But this aide just kept writing, paying no attention to me.

"No," I said, using the one very firm word I know people understand from me. But she kept writing.

"No. No. No!" I repeated.

She continued on as if I hadn't said anything. She made no effort to understand what was wrong, and frankly, I was scared of her. I was worried a lot about not being understood, worried and stressed about that, now that my life was always around people who didn't get me, didn't appreciate that I needed to know what was going on. They didn't help me understand.

The fear in me began to grow. If she didn't understand what was wrong now, what was going to happen when a bigger deal occurred and she didn't understand? So I kind of blew up, doing whatever I had to do get her to stop writing, to get her attention.

She ran out of the apartment, and when the door slammed behind her, it locked her out.

And then the damn police showed up. They were not ready to try to understand a person with limited speech like me. They asked many questions.

"What happened?"

"What's your name?"

"How did the door get locked?"

I couldn't answer any of their questions and felt the panic growing. Their frustration and mine just fed the situation. And then the lady who ran the agency showed up and called my dad. I was so glad when he came to get me. He was safe.

In the days after I left the campus, I was happy to be home, and also sad to have left UCLA. I will admit part of me was pleased. It wasn't my intention to come home but I was much relieved when my parents had me move back. But then, after that, the sadness grew.

Things at UCLA hadn't been perfect. Sometimes it was stressful. The classes were boring. I was often homesick. I didn't feel in sync with the other kids or my classes. My experience at home, meanwhile, had always been so comfortable. My parents understood me so well, they gave me space when I needed it. At UCLA, it was challenging, though I wanted to be there.

In the aftermath, though, I was worried most that my parents would be disappointed in me. Really, I only wanted them to be happy with me.

I also worried about my future. I really had no clue what came next. It was all at the hands of my parents, but I had just put a major bump in the only plan we'd had. I don't want to think they were burdened by me, but they had that hopeless look. I bet they didn't know what came next either.

Then I met Lindsey, I liked her instantly. She just treated me differently than most. I felt good around her.

With Lindsey, I felt like she knew what was inside me and believed in me, and that inspired me to work extra hard. She always spoke directly to me and talked to me as an adult, always validated my feelings. She became very important to me.

Working with her using letter boards, there were times I was so frustrated and she could see it. She was really understanding and would say things like "It must be so frustrating to not be able to say what you're thinking." She understood me. It's not that there was a sudden change when I was no longer

happy being silent. I can't say that I was ever happy being si-
lent, though I was content. Perhaps because it was all I knew.
My whole life was based around the frustrations caused by not
having a say. I didn't know anything else.

When Lindsey first tried to get me to do FC, it felt hard. I
could not really get what she asked of me because it was like
stuff I could answer with words. She had me type my name and
kept it really basic to start. It did not feel like the beginning of
something much bigger.

I didn't really understand what she was trying to get me to
do. She was asking me questions that I knew she had asked be-
fore and I had answered, so why did she now want me to type
it? Like she would say 'what is your name?' and obviously she
knew my name. It wasn't as frustrating as some other things, it
was just confusing.

Lindsey mostly worked with me on speech therapy. We did
a lot of the same things I'd done in other speech therapy ses-
sions and we were not really getting anywhere, but I still made
a lot of effort.

12

Let's talk about my physical stims. Vocal stims are me thinking. Or anger or excitement. Musical ones are me thinking or working.

List of physical stims. The left hand forefinger snapping with right hand next to it. This is my main one. It's so many things but usually frustration. I think maybe it riles me up too much. Like just the act of doing it puts me in a bad or worse place. That's maybe something to work on. It's no good for me.

I'm partly at fault for getting frustrated in the first place. I think it's sometimes autistic child taking over. That's a lot of these stims. That's a problem. I'm not even controlling my own body. I must talk with her. It's the vocal stims and physical too. They're all connected to her juvenile state. This is huge!

Right finger on right ear while making high pitched sounds: it's autistic child thinking. The ear is like touching the brain. She makes the noises to indicate that she's discovered something or made a connection.

Tapping left ear with index finger: this is frustration too.

I literally get mad at myself for my brain not achieving. Some-times it's more than one finger.

Rocking back and forth. This is something about feeling comfortable; rocking is like my security blanket. The motion is like being rocked to sleep.

Hit myself in the head with my left wrist. This is a bad one. It's me wanting to hurt myself for not being normal.

"We'd love to have you, Tom, and Emily come along to Ireland with us." One of the directors at Leaps n Boundz approached me about participating in the overseas adventure they were planning. Leaps n Boundz was a social services agency that provided adaptive sports, recreation, and social programming for individuals with special needs. Emily went to their facility on a regular basis and often enjoyed her time there. It was one of the ways we filled her days after the UCLA debacle.

Much of what the agency provided was funded by grants as well as through the state, but the kind of trip they were planning to Dublin would require families to pay privately.

I loved the idea of an overseas trip with Emily. Here was a chance to show her so much more of the world and to do so within the cocoon of this organization that was used to working with her, who knew her limitations, and who understood her as well as the challenges she could present. We'd travel with a group of thirty, seven of whom were autistic young adults, as well as their families and caregivers. Though all the other autistic clients were only minimally verbal, they still had significantly more verbal language than Emily. She could possibly do it.

Tom had reservations. "It's hard enough managing Emily

at home," he said. "Her meltdowns have become more frequent. What if she gets aggressive overseas? That could be a nightmare. Maybe it's too much to ask of her."

"Wouldn't you like to see Ireland with her? Explore the country? Get out of LA?"

"Of course I would. I just worry."

We went back and forth. The travel agent must have wanted to kill me. I canceled and reinstated our reservation I don't know how many times. I also went to see Dr. Wolf to get a hefty prescription of sedatives to keep Emily calm on the trip. She had a lot of anxiety, some of it caused by her sensory sensitivity. We used the medication cautiously and only as needed to help manage those symptoms.

"Just don't exceed the dosage recommendations," Dr. Wolf said.

"WE'LL BE ON a plane for a long time," I explained to Emily. "We're flying at night and your seat will turn into a bed. You'll probably sleep the whole night away and when you wake up, we'll be in Dublin."

She nodded.

When the day came, Emily was beyond excited. She had known about the trip since its inception and wore a green T-shirt and bandanna in honor of the destination. We met up with the group at the airport and took pictures. She couldn't stop smiling.

Boarding the plane, Emily was entranced with everything, looking, studying, examining. She settled down for dinner, then she got into her pajamas and zonked out. No problem.

In Dublin, we checked into the hotel. Leaps n Boundz brought along an employee with a background in behavior intervention to help out with the group. Her services would be available to us whenever needed. We were ready for our European adventure.

We took a sightseeing tour of the city on an amphibious World War II vehicle known as a duck boat, together with the others from Leaps n Boundz. We learned about Viking-era Dublin, and saw both Saint Patrick's and Christchurch Cathedrals. We viewed Trinity College, government buildings, and Georgian Dublin from the funny-looking conveyance. The climax of the tour was coming, when the duck boat splashed into the water at the Grand Canal docklands near U2's recording studio. I kept looking forward to that part, hoping Emily would enjoy it. I could smell the sea air and braced myself. When our bus-like vehicle plunged into the water, the passengers broke into spontaneous applause so infectious, I couldn't help but join in.

I looked over at Emily. She stared about, impassive, indifferent.

After that, the Leaps staff started gathering the young adults for a visit to a leprechaun museum. The parents were scheduled to tour and sample the goods at the Guinness brewery. Though the plan had been in place all along, in the moment it felt sprung on us as we rode together on a city bus. Our two groups were about to part ways.

I turned to Emily. "We're leaving now, and we're going to . . ." We tried to prepare her, but she and the other kids were all being corralled off the bus. It was abrupt and I could see she was upset.

As our bus pulled away, Emily stood on the curb in

Dublin looking completely bewildered. She was screaming her head off.

There was a lot of screaming during that trip.

"Can you call Aer Lingus and see if we can just go home?" I asked Tom. "I don't think this is going to work."

With our transferrable plane tickets, we had that ace in a hole. If things got bad, we could always go home. Still, we'd come so far. After that curb screaming incident, though, she calmed down. We could give it another chance. Besides, I wanted to see Ireland. I had always wanted to do this trip.

NEXT ON THE itinerary was a trip to Belfast to see where the *Titanic* had been built. Tom came down with a cold and opted to stay in Dublin, so Emily and I went on the bus, a three- or four-hour journey together.

On the ride, she got agitated and started doing her verbal stims and finger flapping. It was disruptive.

One of the kids in the program didn't help matters.

"Is she ever going to stop making noise?" he kept saying. "Is she ever going to stop?"

I'm sure Emily heard him and felt irritated as well.

Meanwhile, I kept talking to her in an effort to calm her. I did not want to use medication. Every time there was a slight change in the itinerary, or a lengthy wait, or strange foods, Emily showed signs of a possible meltdown. I wanted to nip any potential outburst in the bud. Even when I did resort to the use of sedatives, they didn't help, so I stopped. If Emily became agitated, there was little I could do besides talk to her—or simply let her spiral down and move past the upset.

We went on a ghost tour in Kilkenny with a costumed guide who walked us through the streets of the city. Emily went along but wasn't overly interested or impressed. While we didn't have any real problems with her behavior on that tour, I don't know how much she enjoyed it. Walking around Kilkenny, as well as the other cities on the tour, watching the people, taking in the life in this foreign land was what really appealed to her.

Falconry and hurling were also on the agenda. She watched as Tom and I stood with leather-gloved arms to have a hawk land on us, but the falconry made no real impact on her. She tolerated it. The hurling—an outdoor team game of ancient Gaelic Irish origin, in which players use a wooden stick (called a "hurl") to hit a small ball into the opposing team's goal—however, she really enjoyed. Whenever we did things outside with other people, she liked the experience: walking in parks, being around castles, eating in restaurants.

THE HASSLES OF travel, meanwhile, took a toll: sleeping in different places, the constant shuffling about, the unfamiliar sounds, textures, and sights, the crowds and chaos. Emily was a little more anxious and agitated with each passing day.

On the itinerary was one stop that for me was the highlight of the trip, though I know I was kind of silly in my thinking about it. We were going to see Blarney Castle. As everyone knows, kissing the Blarney Stone is said to confer the gift of gab on the kisser. I'm a bit superstitious. Such thinking wasn't logical, but why not? It could happen for her. Kissing that famous stone certainly couldn't hurt. Perhaps Emily would spontaneously receive the gift of speech.

The Blarney Stone is a block of carboniferous limestone that was set into the castle wall in 1446, though the reason it's there and how it gained its reputation for bestowing eloquence on a kisser is a source of much debate. The castle itself is a popular tourist site, attracting visitors from all over the world. Winston Churchill and President William H. Taft were reportedly among the visitors who'd come seeking the gift of gab.

And now, so would Emily Faith Grodin.

To kiss the stone, though, was no easy feat. A person has to be held while they lean backward to reach the stone, essentially upside down. I didn't know how that would go over with Emily.

WHEN WE ARRIVED at Blarney Castle, the place was crawling with tourists. A cruise ship had docked locally and expelled hundreds of sightseers. Our own group was on a tight timetable, tied to a bus schedule. As soon as we got to the castle and saw the lines to kiss the stone, my heart plummeted. I really wanted her to kiss it. We'd come so far. I felt so silly and yet . . .

I stared at the lines of people waiting for their chance. Emily would never put up with standing in that line just to placate me. Even if I could convince her, there just was not time. If there had been, she likely wouldn't tolerate the process of kissing the stone. What about the germs? I was more disappointed than I should have been.

We toured the gardens and the gift shop and the whole time, I felt myself growing bluer and bluer. It was almost time to leave. We needed to go back to the bus. We were about to hit the parking lot when I took Emily by the hand.

"Here, come with me."

Tom followed, unsure of what was up.

"Blarney Stone, Blarney Castle. What difference does it make?" I hustled through the castle grounds. "They could be the same thing, for all we know. Maybe it's the castle that holds the magic."

I led her to a quiet side of the castle, away from all the other tourists, to a slab of rock with streaks of lichen and moss on it.

"Okay, Emily," I said. "Just kiss the castle."

She must have thought I'd lost my mind, as I'm sure Tom did.

I mimed for her what to do.

She did as I asked, laughing, convinced, I'm sure, that I was off my rocker. She did indeed kiss the castle. Did that make the difference? It's so ridiculous to think so. And yet, I'm so glad I insisted.

My favorite part of that trip to Ireland was the glorified version of an overseas trip that I had in my mind, more so than the trip itself. I did enjoy being with my parents on the trip— they are excellent travelers. And the beauty of the environment; I did like to see a world so very different from the one I am in every day. I liked much of the foreignness of the experience, and I was surprised by how different a place could be from my own home. I think the oldness of it all almost felt like going back to another time. It was my first time experiencing something like that.

Still, I was intimidated by a lot of it because I knew from all of the preparation for the trip that it was a big deal. I was so far from home that, even in an emergency, I would not be able to go home. Before we went, I didn't think the flight would be intimidating, but then when I was on it that first time for so many hours. It just went on and on. Like, the intimidation builds and it really takes a toll.

I absolutely wanted to go abroad for the experience, but I did not really have the experience that I was hoping for. I was very disappointed in my inability to make it work better for my parent's sake.

I was happy to be in Ireland in the beginning, and that faded and I really wanted to be home.

13

If having Emily kiss the Blarney Stone is considered a woo-woo ploy by a desperate parent hoping to prove her daughter is more intelligent and capable than is realistic by making sure she's suddenly granted the gift of speech, some in the autism and speech-therapy communities would consider the facilitated communication (FC) we'd been trying unsuccessfully with Lindsey to be just as suspect.

We had first explored FC when Emily was thirteen, but it had had no impact on her. By the time she returned home from UCLA, FC was really the only therapy we still had not exhausted. We had no idea whether it would now be successful and we had no vested interest in making sure this method worked where others had failed. We simply approached FC like many of the therapies we engaged: we would throw it against the wall and see if it stuck.

Alternative and augmentative communication (AAC) is the umbrella term that encompasses many types of communication, including pointing at pictures, letters, or objects, or the use of sign language—and is highly respected and accepted in the autism and disability communities. FC is a form of AAC in which people express themselves by typing on a keyboard, often with the assistance of a communication partner, who may be a teacher, parent, speech pathologist, or a friend.

Often, efforts toward using FC start out with the communication partner offering a letter board, which is like a printed keyboard, usually covered in clear plastic. The partner asks the client to point at letters, one by one, to spell out whatever the partner requests, such as the client's name, the words "cat" or "dog," or the color "red." The partner, meanwhile, provides physical stability to help the client hit the correct keys. The backward resistance offered by the partner, often at the client's elbow, may serve to slow the pace of the client's pointing and/or to help overcome the client's impulsiveness. This support also assists the client to resist striking a target letter repetitively.

The partner is also supposed to provide emotional and communicative support by verbally encouraging and motivating the client. This is especially important as many typers experience high levels of anxiety. In addition, the partner provides communicative support to help the client stay focused and to clarify ambiguous messages. For example, if the client stops in the middle of a sentence, the partner might say, "Do you want to finish that thought?" or read back the sentence to lure the client into the headspace that had been present at the origination of the thought. In doing so, the partner communicates respect and the presumption of the client's competence.

Later, after Emily's breakthrough, when I thought more deeply about the support that Lindsey would provide, it made total sense. If Emily's limitations were rooted in issues of movement and timing, then having a partner who could offer stability and make up for these movement and timing-based shortcomings might help.

This is what Emily later had to say about working with her communication partner: *My partner offers support in so many ways. My emotional control is weak. I need that help to be able to organize my thoughts and when emotion is added I go into panic mode. I am the kind of person, who when given a task, will work through even if a break would be beneficial. My partners have helped me to recognize this for myself because otherwise I would again work myself into a panic.*

TRAINING OFFERED IN FC by Syracuse University's Institute on Communication and Inclusion clearly states that the communication partner should never move or lead the person.

The partner is there to provide support, not to influence the conversation. Apparently, though, that wasn't always the case and that, unfortunately, led to the discrediting of the technique.

Today, if you Google FC, you'll absorb a heavy dose of caution mixed with the fear of fraud—which I get. Over time, too many people in the autism community have been taken in by shady and untenable ideas that thrive on a parent's desperate hope that their child may have some kind of miraculous breakthrough. Of course there should be caution. The same is true in the cancer community and elsewhere when hope is the coin of the realm. Still, there are good reasons to examine the criticism in order to understand it better.

Over the years, several highly publicized instances of autistic persons producing sophisticated responses were later shown to be false. The communication partner, it was found, had in fact "led" the autistic individual to produce the answer, often by placing their own hand over the autistic person's hand. In some cases, the partner had done this leading without realizing it—had, in essence, produced "the Ouija Board effect." Called the hand-over-hand method, it has since been eliminated in the proper practice of FC.

Then there was the headline-grabbing case of Anna Stubblefield, a professor of ethics at Rutgers University who served as a communication partner with a man who had cerebral palsy. "With his hand in hers, she helped him type out words after nearly 30 years of silence," reported the *New York Times Magazine* in their exposé. Stubblefield fell in love with the man and believed her affections were reciprocated, and thus started a sexual relationship with him. The family believed differently and had her arrested. Initially, Stubblefield was convicted on two counts of first-degree aggravated assault against the man because, it was argued, he was not capable of giving consent. Eventually, the case was overturned and she pled guilty to a lesser charge, but the damage to FC was done.

However, the notion that *all* FC is impossible because of the Stubblefield case, or because of several cases in which results were manipulated, is unconvincing and as dangerous as the categorically opposite view. Think of it like cancer treatments: just because a particular treatment only works for some patients doesn't mean no one should receive it.

One of the most maddening positions against FC is based on dubious and frankly arrogant logic that goes like this: Because certain autistic individuals are capable of doing things that appear to be the equivalent of independent typing—

turning on and playing a video game, for example—why would they need the typing "support" and physical proximity of the communication partner to communicate? That is, why can't they just do it on their own? However, this way of thinking fails to take into consideration the very neurological and sensory challenges that often characterize individuals with autism. Indeed, it plays into the downright untrue notion that those on the autism spectrum, particularly those who lack oral speech, are cognitively limited and should be considered intellectually disabled. As wrong as these conclusions are, and despite the evidence of so many, including Emily, demonstrating significantly high levels of intelligence and insight through the use of FC, the dismissal of the methodology by its critics was largely clinched by Stubblefield and other high-profile cases, leading to numerous doctors and speech therapists coming out publicly against it.

Since then, many large and influential associations like the American Speech-Language-Hearing Association (ASHA) have used these cases to disparage FC, effectively taking a hardened stance that has made it more difficult for many with autism who might benefit from gaining access. If disability rights are all about granting individuals dignity and choice, this frozen position is, to some of us, infuriating.

A few years ago ASHA released a statement saying that facilitated communication was "a discredited technique that should not be used." Pushback came fast and with fury. On July 17, 2018, a national coalition of twenty-three civil and disability rights organizations called on ASHA to withdraw its statement, asserting that the consequences of its position would "almost certainly lead to civil rights violations." The opposition was motivated by a community that deeply desires to believe in FC. The coalition claimed that ASHA's position was flawed because, among other reasons, it was based on the unfounded and discriminatory presumption that people with speech-related disabilities are incapable of complex thought. Further, ASHA's statement was developed behind closed doors without input from users, professionals, or ASHA members who have experience with the method.

Despite the controversies, though, FC has continued to flourish because in some cases—certainly not all—it provides a real and very tangible form of communication for individuals who have no other outlet. Syracuse University, the University of Kansas, and the University of New Hampshire, among others, continue to research FC and consider it a legitimate field of study.

There's no question that FC does not work for everyone. However, it's yet another tool that should be considered for those who have limited verbal communication. For Emily and many with limited or impaired speech, movement regulation issues, and/or difficulty initiating language, FC has proved helpful.

In May 2020, a small-scale peer-reviewed study was released in *Scientific Reports* looking at the question of whether communications produced via FC are the actual thoughts of the people typing. Using head-mounted eye-tracking devices on nonspeaking autistic people, the study investigated what they called the typers' "communicative agency"—attempting to discern if the typer was the one conveying the thoughts, not the communication partner. The study found that the cuing of the participants' performance was "unlikely."

"The speed, accuracy, timing, and visual fixation patterns

suggest that participants pointed to letters they selected themselves, not letters they were directed to by the assistant." Thus, the study concluded, "the blanket dismissal of assisted autistic communication is therefore unwarranted."

THIS IS WHAT Emily has to say to ASHA:

PRONOUNCEMENTS AND DENOUNCEMENTS

Make light of my condition
Partake in the derision
Not a word to me you've said
Yet you purport to know what is in my head
I ply you with typing
You respond with griping
People outside don't know
How low you can go
The timing is just right
For my triumphs to be out of your sight
That is the nature of the beast
Who chooses always to see the least
Friends though they appear to be
To me they are the enemy
Having people support my expression
To you your power it will lessen
Change your fear
Because soon my independence will be clear

14

THE UNSPOKEN STORM WITHIN

I have felt the storm within me. The storm of things unsaid.
The crippling weight of thoughts
Emotions
Opinions
That can't quite make it to the surface.
I have had to find other ways. Other ways to make them heard.
Ways to let the world see that I am thinking, and breathing, and experiencing just as the rest.
My mind is a constant whirlwind, pondering rapidly on everything, and nothing.
Musing in my own head, locked away, the best kept secret under the circumstances.
That is, my circumstances.
A polite way of saying she doesn't speak. She can't form her words in such a necessary way, the same way our lungs need oxygen to expand and breathe.
Her joy, her grief, the elated chatters of a young girl, buried, trapped.

And in these unspoken words, a storm brews.
It raises in strength and intensity, needing escape, craving to live in the real world.
But all that emits are tiny fragments, little drops that only tell an inch of the mile going on inside.
All that the world will hear is laughter or screams or sounds they can't interpret.
And how can I provide more? How can I begin to portray the tiny details and specifics, when my words cannot paint the big picture.
I am left with the storm, just me and the storm.
I am left with the words unspoken, just me and the unspoken words
The questions and ideas that form, I am left eternally within the storm.
One would think it a treasure, the time and space to contemplate long and thoroughly, like a philosophy spoken inside, well practiced and never too soon.
But what good are they, known solely by me, me and the storm?

We were trapped at 36,000 feet on the transatlantic Aer Lingus jet filled with 273 passengers, three-quarters of the way home to Los Angeles. It was August 2016. Because the trip over had been a piece of cake, I was unprepared for what was now occurring.

Things had started to turn on us back before boarding in the Dublin airport. I'd taken my shoes off to go through security and smashed my foot on something hard and metal. My little toe immediately turned black and blue; it was completely inflamed and swollen. I thought I might have broken it. I hobbled onto the plane.

"My daughter has autism," I explained to the flight

attendant as we were seated. "She sometimes has issues and episodes. I want to warn you in case."

He couldn't have been nicer. "Oh, I know. I have a nephew with autism. Sometimes they have their fits. It's nothing to worry about it." He even brought ice for my toe.

Once the plane took off, I realized I was in trouble regarding food. For some reason, on the flight over there'd been menu choices that would appeal to Emily. Now, though, as I read through the options for this flight, I realized she'd have trouble with just about everything offered. Usually I carry food for her just in case, but I hadn't brought anything this time. I only had junk food—chips and cookies—in my bag. It was going to be a ten-hour flight. This wouldn't do.

I called another attendant over and explained the situation. "Do you have, like pasta or something kind of plain she can eat?" The flight attendant managed to find a pasta meal that had been ordered but not claimed. Perfect.

Because she'd slept most of the journey on the flight over, I hadn't then noticed the little privacy screens between the seats. We were in business class where the seats recline into beds, and now, with the screen between my seat and Emily's, I couldn't easily get around it to see how or what she was doing. We were flying in the middle of the day, so she didn't want to sleep. I tried to get her to listen to music, to put on headphones, to watch a video. Anything to make the time go by faster, but she wouldn't do anything I suggested. She sat there, almost totally immobile, staring at the blank video monitor in front of her. Hour after hour after hour.

"How about I put the bed down for you and you can take a nap?" I tried.

"No."

She made little noises, occasionally flipping her fingers in front of her eyes. As time went on, the noises got louder and more frequent, as did the finger motions. She showed all the precursors of an episode. I tried every trick in the book to forestall the brewing storm. I gave her a sedative. It hadn't helped much in Ireland, but it was all I had.

By the eighth hour, two hours before we were scheduled to land in Los Angeles, the dam burst. Emily's screaming started. Her meltdown was audible to just about every passenger on that plane. She screamed at the top of her voice. Children near us look terrified and cowered. Adults appeared either scared or annoyed. The behavioral aide from Leaps, seated in coach, attempted to come into business class to help—she'd clearly heard Emily's distress from the back of the plane—but the attendants wouldn't let her through. They didn't understand the situation. Meanwhile, the airline attendants in business class kept asking me to calm her. I'd already given her what I could.

The hardest part was this: she was miserable as well. She'd rather not be having a meltdown on a plane at 36,000 feet; I knew this with every fiber of my being. She'd rather not be autistic. She'd like to have a way to communicate with us. And if she could communicate, meltdowns like this might be a thing of the past.

I remembered Tom's reluctance to take this trip, the way we'd scheduled and canceled flights, driving the travel agent crazy. Do we? Don't we? Not knowing if she was able or if this was a good move for her. Had I been wrong to insist?

Now here we were, stuck with hours to go before we'd touch down, with Emily screaming, flapping her fingers, hitting herself, drawing the eyes of everyone on the plane. She was twenty-five, no longer a child. Her physical presence was big enough to call major attention. Her loud voice could be frightening, and her agitated movements sometimes looked like aggression. I wanted to crawl under the seat.

AFTER ABOUT FORTY-FIVE minutes, the worst of the screaming subsided. She was never fully quiet again on the plane, but eventually it wasn't as bad as it had initially been. After we landed and collected our luggage, my brother picked us up. It was 6:00 p.m. on a Friday night in LA, the height of rush-hour traffic.

"We'll tell you about the trip later," I said to him the minute we got in the car to forestall any questions. "Let's just get home."

Emily started screaming again and kept it up most of the drive. I kept thinking, *I'll never get on another fucking plane with her ever again.* When I whispered that to Tom, he said, "I want that on tape."

We were wrecked, all of us. And frankly, I wasn't sure it had been worth it. The truth was, no matter what we did, Emily hadn't participated in much. She went along because she almost always goes along, but I don't think she loved the trip. I was exhausted and sorry I'd pushed for it.

There is a moment of clarity before a meltdown hits. Like peace before the chaos that I would give anything to hang onto. But it slips violently through my grasp like a fleeting rope in a lost game of Tug-O-War, leaving me standing, hands stung, defeated. I am powerless. My mind in that moment bellows louder than my voice ever could. If only I would listen to my-self. My mind pleads with my body but to no avail.

"You don't need to scream," I tell myself. "You can be the one in control." Yet despite my own best efforts, the tornado touches down. I am forced to surrender to the violent storm.

"Maybe there's something you can give her?" I hear the flight attendant ask my mom. "Something to calm her down."

"She's already taken enough." Mom's voice has the polite directness I know so well. "It's not safe to give her more." She's trying to rein in the situation, but I've made quite a scene. And it looks like I'm not done yet.

I start to wonder if the attendant thinks they'll have to land the plane, that my meltdown has gotten so out-of-control that that's the only option. Fuck. Would they really land the plane? I can't believe they would really do that, but I worry.

I've had my meltdowns in the past, but this—this is a new level of chaos. Hitting myself really makes me look crazy. I know that.

People sit, some stuck facing my direction. I know they want to look away but they can't. My screaming and aggressive body movements don't help. I wish I could stop it. I feel the heat of their stares drawn to me like a magnet.

I enjoyed the expedition. The days of traveling in Ireland were interesting but also overwhelming. This was my first trip abroad. My last, too, I'm sure, after this. And who could blame my parents? They put up with so much.

I'd been excited to go and there were many good moments, but they're all backed up inside of me now. I am full to the brim with emotions and words and all that's going on in my head and I have no outlet for all of it. Plus I'm stuck on this plane, everybody looking at me. I can't get away, can't find a way to calm myself.

I am a goddamn car accident.

15

"I almost called to cancel." I ushered Lindsey into the house for her regular appointment with Emily the next morning and told her about the difficult flight. "Let's give it a try and see if today's session works out. Getting back to normal will help. It's been a tough patch for all of us."

We were utterly wrung out. That flight home had wiped out whatever reserves we'd had. When I'd woken that morning I hadn't wanted to get out of bed. That was not like me. I couldn't simply blame the jet lag. Something else was going on. I'd descended into one of the lowest points I'd ever experienced, as a parent, as a human. I never wanted to go through another flight like that again.

That morning, it took everything I had to put one foot in front of the other, I was so swamped with sadness and regret. Over the years I'd experienced melancholy and sorrow about our situation. I'd been angry and outraged and knocked low and unhappy. This was different. For the first time, I felt hopeless. After all we'd done, there'd been no payoff. Maybe there was never going to be a payoff. I didn't want to keep moving forward; I didn't want to take the next breath.

Frankly, I didn't even want to interact with Emily. Her agitation was too much to be around. Tom had had reservations about taking this trip, so for me, its abject failure felt like a personal defeat. He didn't say "I told you so," but he had warned me and I hadn't listened. I was defeated and looked like a fool. Yet once again, I'd made the wrong decision in my effort to give her every opportunity.

LINDSEY AND EMILY settled on the couch, this time with an iPad between them. Lindsey had recently tried the tablet in her work with Emily to see if that made any difference getting her to respond. So far, no change. Occasionally Emily would type one word. More often, nothing.

I busied myself, determined to keep moving forward. As soon as Lindsey started the session, though, things went sideways. Almost immediately, Emily became agitated. Her screaming began in earnest, filling the house. I wanted to crawl under the floorboards, to run away, to be anywhere but where I was, in this life I'd been given. Other mothers didn't have to go through all this. Other marriages weren't strained in this way. Why me? Why us? After that awful flight yesterday, I had no ability to absorb this new breakdown. I was done.

Emily started to hit herself in the head with her fists, one after another, pummeling her skull as she squealed and cried. *Here we go again.* I needed it to stop. Certainly, the fact that we were home should have made a difference. It was time for a break from all this.

Tom and I had never before experienced such a deep sense of defeat. I couldn't keep going. I was so tired of this path.

"I got this crushing feeling inside," Tom said later. "Oh my God: *How much more of this can I take?* Her screams hurt, like I was being jabbed in the stomach."

"Maybe we should cancel for today," I said to Lindsey.

"Don't worry," she assured us, shooing us away. "I've got this."

"Come on, Tom," I said, relieved that Lindsey was going to help. "Let's go upstairs and unpack."

Lindsey was a pro and busy working to redirect Emily with an article about astronomy and planets. She read the article aloud to Emily, and then, as Emily calmed, Lindsey asked her questions. From upstairs where I fought the urge to crawl back into bed and make this day go away, I could hear the session continue and the meltdown subside. They were talking about stars and planets; and serenity was returning.

"What is floating in space?" Lindsey asked.

Emily typed a basic response: *rocks and dust*

"A small rock is called a . . . ?" prompted Lindsey.

pebble, wrote Emily.

"And a big rock?"

boulder

The upset quieted. Tom and I unpacked from Ireland. Soon, though, it was simply too quiet downstairs. Emily often makes verbal sounds, a kind of singsong cadence you could play on a piano. Now, she wasn't making any sounds at all. Tom and I looked at each other. Something was up. I couldn't hear Lindsey asking her questions, either, which was odd. Emily had been highly agitated only a few minutes earlier. She didn't usually quiet down that fast and that easily.

Tom left the bedroom to go downstairs to check. I was on his heels.

He was two stairs down when he almost collided with Lindsey, running up the stairs, holding the iPad. I joined them on the landing. Lindsey's eyes filled with tears as she thrust the iPad into my hands.

"We just had a breakthrough. Read this."

I feel very bad when I hurt people.

I looked at Lindsey, trying to understand. Was she saying that Emily had written this complete sentence, about how she felt inside? That wasn't possible.

"She typed that?" I asked.

Lindsey nodded, too overwhelmed to speak.

Doctors and therapists and experts of all kinds had warned us that Emily would likely never communicate with us in the way we wanted. They'd cautioned that we shouldn't expect to ever know what was going on inside her. Was I seeing only what I wanted to see?

I read the next line.

I want to tell you the thoughts I have never allowed out and thought they never would be. Now I'm certain I'll be heard.

"What happened?" I asked Lindsey.

"I read to her and asked her questions, and she wrote one-word answers. Then, she just sort of looked at the keyboard, hunched over it, and began typing. Like, *really* typing."

Emily wanted to communicate. She wanted to talk to us. I was floored, but also on guard.

Much of our work as parents has been in accepting and loving Emily exactly as she was and not wishing she was somehow different. Every dream for my daughter might now have reason to spread its wings. I wasn't sure if this could even be real. If I allowed myself to believe it was real, if I let in the possibility that Emily might yet tell me about her inner life, I would be crushed if I found out it wasn't true. And yet I wanted it to be real more than I needed to take the next breath.

Emily's words on the iPad continued:

I have been buried under years of dust. Just found my voice. And now I have so much to say. I want you to hear me by reading my words. All the hard work will pay off now.

I was breathless and didn't really understand what I was looking at. It wasn't possible. It couldn't be. Perhaps Lindsey had noticed our distress and, in her desire to ease life for us, had inadvertently guided Emily into writing words that were not really hers. Because, really, it made no sense that in one instant the impossible had suddenly become possible. I wanted to believe that Emily had experienced a genuine breakthrough, the kind we'd long dreamed of, but I wasn't sure.

All these thoughts swirled as we stood on the landing, looking down at Emily seated on the couch. Our twenty-five-year-old daughter. Our beautiful, intelligent, deeply loved daughter. Please God, let it be real. We looked at her, shaking our heads in delighted disbelief and wonder, unsure of what was what.

Emily turned to look up at us on the stairs. Her face broke into a huge smile. She nodded at us as if to say, *Yes, it's real. I'm here. I'm ready.*

Finally back in Los Angeles, nothing feels like home. The air in the house is heavy with exhaustion. All at once, something inside me awakens amidst my regular Tuesday session with my communication therapist and I am present in this moment. Years have brought countless treatments, therapies, you name it I've tried it.

When you're autistic everyone thinks they can fix you. I don't think I have ever felt like I needed to be fixed as much as I needed to be understood. Never seeing a way out of the haze, I fell inside myself. Collapsed were my ambitions while my fears refused to rest. I'm surprised by this overwhelming desire to find a voice, my voice.

Carefully I approach the letters on the keyboard unsure if this could work yet desperate to find a way out.

The amount of energy it took to point to each letter in order to spell out even a single word was astounding. The exhilaration of putting my thought down in a way that someone else could understand lifted me off the ground. It started with answers to questions about something altogether arbitrary. The questions then turned to me and I did something extraordinary. I answered them. Never again will I bury my voice. Never again will I be silent.

As it turned out, she *was* ready to communicate, though it took some time for us to ascertain what was real from what we simply hoped for. We took her to her psychiatrist, Dr. Wolf, to have the doctor assess what was happening.

"When you first told me you were working with this kind of facilitated communication thing, I frankly thought, *Poor people. They've tried everything and now they've got some person moving her arm around and they believe she's typing. Oh my God, how could they go for that?*" Dr. Wolf later told me, recounting those initial visits after Emily had started typing.

Her impression quickly changed, though, when I came

into her office with Emily and Lindsey. "Then it was so crazy," Dr. Wolf said, remembering.

Emily was sitting across from Dr. Wolf and Lindsey was just touching her shoulder. "And Emily's like—slowly, because she does it with one finger—typing all her answers to me on the iPad," Dr. Wolf said.

Some of Emily's answers, the doctor remembered, were really funny. For instance, there'd been talk of Emily wanting to move in with Lindsey.

"How are you going to feel if you can make this move?" Dr. Wolf asked her.

"'Well, my parents have been doing this a long time and I really think they need a vacation from me,' and then she starts to laugh," Dr. Wolf recounted.

The doctor told me that when she questioned Emily about her medications, Emily was able to respond in enormous detail about how she felt about each, and what was helping her and what wasn't.

"[I could ask her] all the questions I've wanted to ask her but have never been able to," Dr. Wolf said. She even asked Emily about the incident at UCLA and was amazed by her answer. Emily told her that she'd been so upset that night "'because they thought I was stupid and they treated me like I wasn't there. And I was so angry about how they looked at me and they would just try to make me do something.' Emily didn't feel like people were treating her like a person—and it's so compelling for her to be able to actually say that and put these kinds of things together," said Dr. Wolf.

Was there any way we were misguided into thinking Emily was really writing to us? Had we somehow led the witness, and Lindsey was unconsciously helping her? I asked.

"Anytime I've seen Emily type, she is actually the one that has the iPad," Dr. Wolf said. "She has it on her lap on a pillow that I gave her and she's doing it herself. And the only time I've seen Lindsey intervene is if Emily suddenly stops, like she's in the middle of answering something and has paused. Lindsey will say, 'Go on.' And then Emily will just continue what she's doing."

Dr. Wolf reminded me that there were questions she asked that only Emily would know how to answer, medical-related queries about specific medications.

"For example, I changed one of her medications, from Valium to Xanax," she said. "So I asked Emily about the difference between them. Emily said, 'The new medicine doesn't last as long. And I find myself more irritable and you know, it doesn't work for me.' It's true that the Xanax doesn't last as long. And it's not as soothing as the Valium." Those were questions Lindsey couldn't have known the answers to.

We'd tried facilitated communication before. Why did it work this time, and not previously?

"I don't know. She might've had so much stuff going on, or maybe the person didn't do it right, or teach it right, or maybe the person was touching her too much and it turned her off. It could have been a lot of different things that were bothering Emily that would foreclose that working, you know?"

She thought for a moment. "There's a certain amount of people who are on the autistic spectrum that have very low IQs. They are not going to be able to communicate no matter how you're going to work with them, because they don't have that built-in capacity. It's just not going to happen. And that really has nothing to do with this kind of facilitated communication. Anyone teaching them to read, or any other task like that, is going to fall flat. In Emily's case, though, she was always very attentive to people reading to her."

It could be that Emily had been understanding a lot over the years, the doctor speculated, learning from books and such. Maybe she had the intellectual makeup needed and the preparation with all that reading we'd done had laid the groundwork, those elements all adding up.

"I don't think that every single person who is autistic could learn how to do this, and I don't think that every single provider of facilitated communication would be calibrated enough to treat every single person who could learn. But I definitely think that it's something that needs to be tried more often in the right circumstances."

Dr. Wolf said she fully believed that Emily was typing her own thoughts, as did others who'd seen her. However, she continued, "because of the controversy around facilitated communication and a lot of unfortunate high-profile cases . . ." Her voice trailed off. "One has to be careful about suggesting this as a way out, or a cure. It's not a cure, not a pathway to communication for many, many people. It's a really small number of incredibly intelligent people who are saddled with autism that this might work for. Does that make sense?"

The doctor paused. "I guess what I'm driving at is that Emily is extraordinary."

16

EVERYTHING SINCE THEN

Everything since then has been somewhat of a dream,
Something like walking in the shoes of a girl different from me.
And the days that led me to this exact point,
They have reason to stain my memory and disrupt my emotion.
But I cannot deny
And cannot claim
That everything since then
Would not be the same
Had those moments not happened,
Though sometimes with tears down my face,
And the bubbling inside that pours into rage,
It's just that some days
Have led to everything since then.
And I would not be me if it wasn't for her,
The girl who was silenced and hadn't yet heard
Of the things that were waiting on just the other side
Of frustration and anger and confusion inside.
That eventually there could be another way,
A better way to say what you need to say
That doesn't involve a landed plane

Or red and blue lights
And feeling afraid.
Because everything since then
Is when life really begins
The everything that couldn't be
If it hadn't gone that way for me.
If I hadn't lived those struggles and times
That clearly state and clearly define
A human with too much to say
Who clearly doesn't have a way.
But it's okay.
It's okay.
Because of everything since then.

"How many times a week can you be here?" I'd asked Lindsey before she left us the day of Emily's breakthrough. Up to that point, she'd worked with Emily an hour a week.

"How many do you need?" Lindsey was as excited as we were. "I'm in."

We couldn't book her often enough. Three times a week, four if possible, an hour and a half each time. Soon we were able to book her for entire Fridays as well.

WHEN I WAS young, I'd learned to write with "invisible ink," which was really just lemon juice diluted with water. I'd dab a cotton swab in the mixture and write a message on white paper. When the liquid dried, the paper looked blank and plain. Give that sheet to someone else and tell them to view the secret message by holding the page to a lamp, light bulb, or heat source, and then the message would reveal itself as if the paper itself were enchanted.

To watch Emily type was to see that same kind of magic being pulled from thin air before our eyes. It was mesmerizing, words and thoughts appearing where before there had been none—and no possibility of words. Tom and I sat behind the couch in the den where Emily and Lindsey were seated. Though typically Lindsey would prime Emily by reading a news article, this day, the first time we watched her type, she started out with a basic question. "How are you today?"

I feel happy because now I can talk.

I am beautiful now that a window in my mind has opened so my dreams can come to fruition.

"What are your dreams?" Lindsey asked.

going to college to study revolutionary ideas around autism. to communicate in everyday life with the people I meet and my family.

"Any other dreams?"

to be calmer and less noisy when I'm upset. that would need to happen.

On the iPad, words and sentences appeared with such insight and knowledge, it was hard to believe. Prior to this moment, I'd had really no specific expectations of what it would be like to see my daughter communicate, but this was beyond my imagination. My eyes burned, straining to see each letter materialize, sentences and phrases that kept scrolling. I was awed. An actual conversation was taking place.

Tom was also stunned. "I'd always hoped she'd communicate with us, but I never could have imagined she'd do so on such a level," he said later. "This was absolutely mind-blowing. To watch Emily produce these words: it was off the charts for me."

Her spelling was perfect, making clear how much she'd been absorbing all along. She'd had an excellent English teacher in high school who'd drilled the kids on grammar and spelling. Clearly, Emily had been paying attention, absorbing the teaching, and learning. Initially, she didn't capitalize the beginnings of sentences nor the personal pronoun "I," but that soon changed. Her grammar was impeccable and her vocabulary astounded me. *Revolutionary ideas around autism . . . a window in my mind has opened . . .* These were not only big concepts well expressed, but done so with a lyric flare. She was being metaphorical.

I ASKED LINDSEY to stick around one day after her session with Emily.

"What do you remember about the day she started typing?" I asked. "I'm still trying to understand."

"She just completely went off the article and said, 'I want to talk. I want to communicate. You've been coming and I haven't been doing it and now I'm ready.'"

"Were you surprised?" I asked. I had been completely astounded and was still not sure what to make of it all. I wanted Lindsey to give me permission to believe.

"That was the first time, for me personally, that anyone had had that kind of breakthrough," Lindsey said. She'd already been working with Emily for six months and thought she knew what she could expect from her. When she'd bounded up the stairs to meet us, iPad in hand, she'd been overwhelmed. I clearly remembered her eyes tearing up when she handed me the iPad.

Up to that point, Emily hadn't been making progress. If Lindsey asked a question that could be answered with a yes or no choice, she was just going to type simply yes or no. If

Lindsey asked something like "Do you prefer potato chips or cookies?" she would type the last option Lindsey had given her, whatever it was, regardless of her preference.

"So why?" I asked. After all the therapies, all the experts, all the interventions, what had made the difference?

"Emily has a lot of life skills and self-care skills that you don't always see in individuals on the spectrum," Lindsey explained. "She was encouraged to be as independent as possible. Plus, take into account all the exposure to the larger world she's had."

It was true. We had encouraged her to be independent and had built her skills to move in that direction. She had been a full and complete participant in the greater world her whole life.

"Think about it," Lindsey continued. "Compare Emily to someone the same age who spent their entire educational career in a special education class. They might learn life skills and the calendar and that kind of stuff, but they'd be in a completely different place psychologically and emotionally than someone like Emily.

"You and Tom always read her books. You put her in general education classes," Lindsey continued. "You and Tom basically said, 'We don't know what's going on, but we see a light in her eyes that tells us she's with us. We're just going to treat her like she deserves that education just like anybody else.' That made a difference."

It was gratifying to hear Lindsey say that, though I won't take the credit. Truly, it was Emily who pushed for this breakthrough.

I've thought a lot about this question since and have come to realize that Emily started typing that day simply because

Emily decided to. She has always done things at her own pace, when she was ready. I couldn't make her do anything. I never could. Give her the opportunity, though, and she may decide to take the next step, just like she walked across the room on her first birthday. Things changed because Emily decided they needed to.

IT WAS ALSO clear how sharply she'd been paying attention to our lives. She wrote about my mother, who was developing dementia. Emily's insight into what was happening, and her deep empathy for the situation, were clear.

LADY AT THE KITCHEN TABLE

Late in the afternoon
When the sun peaks through and almost splits the room in half.
She emerges.
Floats through the room like a weightless balloon caught on a soft
current of air from an open window.
Some may call her frail,
Wrinkled lines and thinning skin,
But in her bright eyes there is a strength.
Hope and confidence still upright in a sea of blue waves eager to
turn this vessel over,
She will not be moved.
The room fills with sweetness,
Roses freshly trimmed,
Warm cookies dipped in milk.
Her soft hands embrace a cup of tea,
Warmth engulfs her face as she lowers to sip.
All of long memories will fade with the steam,

A puzzled look settles in.
What's been home for forty years now unfamiliar,
Glances around the room become as rapid as her beating heart.
She moans a desperate sigh,
Sadness pouring like the pitcher overturned splashes milk onto the
  floor.
Her brightness has faded just enough,
Each time a little more.
She awakens but was never asleep,
Lifts from her wooden chair her thin frame and stands tall.
Perhaps another cup of tea.

I'd seen autistic typers before and they tended to give primarily information and data—what they liked to eat, color or clothes preferences, dislikes—and they always presented the material in a very literal way, not with this kind of deep self-awareness coupled with expressive prose. Even in my work as an advocate for special needs individuals in which I'd encountered many typers, I'd never seen the kind of imaginative and evocative writing come from someone who appeared to have profound limitations.

She also wanted to go to college. I didn't know if that was possible, but we would pull out all the stops to make it happen if that was her dream.

The physical reality of her typing was also startling to observe, like watching someone engaged with a Herculean effort. Her shoulders hunched to the task. The amount of strength, concentration, and effort required to get a single word out was visible. Sometimes, when she finished a thought, she collapsed back in the couch, worn out from the strenuous endeavor. She still made her noises, but they tended to quiet as she worked.

We didn't want to exhaust her by making her type all the

time, but we did want to know everything: What did she think of this life she was living? What did we not know about her? Whatever our questions, Emily wanted to answer us.

That said, it's not like once she started typing daily life evolved into a study in perfection. Lindsey came to work with Emily on a regular basis as Emily gave us more access to her inner life, but the autistic meltdowns still occurred, often amid these typing sessions. When they did, Lindsey redirected her. This one day, Lindsey tried to focus Emily with an article about coal mining. Once the outburst had passed and Emily was concentrating again, Lindsey asked her what had caused the disturbance.

I am not going fast enough.

During a conversation about coal mining, Emily slipped in bits of her perception.

Glad you came, she wrote to Lindsey, . . . *back breaking work . . . this is just hard.*

I didn't know if the "backbreaking work" referred to the coal miners or her strenuous efforts at communication, but clearly, getting her thoughts across was a labor.

THE NEXT TIME Lindsey came over, they discussed sunflowers, and Emily expressed her gratitude, a theme that came up over and over in her writing.

I am thankful for really being able to open the lines of communication.

"What image comes to your mind when you hear 'sunflowers'?" Lindsey asked.

I see a field covered in yellow and green flowers facing the sun.

"Can you tell me about your noises?"

I make them when I feel total havoc in my body and that beats hurting myself.

"Does anything help you?"

Going for a short walk helps me to find peace.

"When is a walk most helpful? In the moment you're upset or at a different time?"

Its best in the morning with dad.

We'd often hoped that those walks she'd shared with Tom had been important to her, and now we found out they were. It was gratifying to know. Soon, though, she became upset again and started to scream and hit herself. Lindsey worked to transfer her attention away from what was upsetting her to a neutral topic. When Emily calmed, Lindsey questioned her.

"Can you tell us what you're feeling?"

Maybe i'm not doing well with all these thoughts. Not an under taking i could have imagined in my life time due to a mountain of struggle you came not a minute too soon.

I couldn't help but look at Emily in a different way now. All the years I'd insisted that someone deep and connected to us was hidden within her. Now here she was, letting us see her in the light of day.

A WEEK OR so later, Emily and I went to Whole Foods where a young employee recognized Emily and said hello. They'd been classmates at Birmingham High School. Emily couldn't stop smiling after that encounter.

When she got home and had her communication partner with her, I asked, "What was going on at Whole Foods?"

It was nice to be recognized by my face, she wrote, *and not my perceived disability.*

I was moved. Yes, I can see how she felt, to always be

known as the autistic girl rather than just Emily. This former classmate had seen Emily as herself. Being able to communicate that to us increased her self-confidence, made the good feelings spread.

"Can you see yourself having conversations with people like that?" Lindsey asked.

Yes, by next year I hope to be walking around with a new voice.

"Why don't we type some more now to warm up your new voice."

Emily, however, demurred. *Anxiety makes my hands heavy.*

She typed regularly and willingly, but sometimes, it was a lot. We respected that and backed off.

TOM AND I were ecstatic with this breakthrough. Still, it was also a period of questioning and disbelief. We weren't sure if this was real. Given all the controversies surrounding FC, I needed to be sure.

Whenever Lindsey came to work with Emily, Tom or I stayed in the room with them, not only to hear firsthand our daughter's thoughts as they were read aloud by the iPad—we had downloaded an app that read her words one by one after she typed them, and when she came to the end of a sentence, spoke aloud the whole thought—but also to verify with our own eyes that what we were seeing was actually happening. We needed to make sure that Lindsey wasn't somehow touching Emily's hands, manipulating her.

Initially, Lindsey gave Emily physical support by cradling Emily's right elbow in her hand, giving a little backward pressure that provided physical stability that Emily needed to push through to type. Other times, as Emily progressed toward independent typing, Lindsey held just a piece of Emily's blouse near her upper arm and nudged her to begin. Occasionally Lindsey didn't touch Emily with her hand at all, but simply sat next to her, pressing the side of her foot against Emily's foot to spur her. With that slight pressure, Emily would type.

Every so often, when Emily's typing slowed or stopped, Lindsey prompted her verbally. "What do you think about that? Can you tell me more?" She also provided emotional support and encouragement.

Most of the time, Emily did tell us more.

I WOKE UP in the middle of the night regularly, perplexed by what was happening. I still wasn't sure it was real, even with Dr. Wolf's assurances. Tom questioned it, too.

"Is this really happening?" I asked

"I think so."

"I'm scared to believe."

"Me, too."

We could see the change in Emily's demeanor; she was clearly happier. The meltdowns weren't gone, but they were becoming less severe and much less frequent.

There was no doubt that the voice we were hearing was Emily's, but still, Tom and I had uncertainties and worried I might have convinced myself to believe in a delusion.

Tom's uncertainties had begun waning during the times he'd watched Emily type. He was mostly retired at this time and able to be around during many of the sessions with Lindsey.

"On the third or fourth time Emily typed with Lindsey," Tom recalled, "Emily was telling her about having attended Shabbat in the Park, what we'd done over the weekend. After the session, Lindsey asked me, 'What's Shabbat?' I knew, then, that the words could only be Emily's. Lindsey didn't even know what Shabbat was."

BEFORE HER BREAKTHROUGH, Emily had met Brendan at an end-of-summer party for the participants in her Saturday dance class; he was a friend of one of her classmates and a few years older. At their first meeting, he'd walked around the room staring at her, following her, clearly smitten. He later invited her to attend his birthday celebration. It was sweet and I assumed she'd have a good time at the party.

However, when we picked her up, she got in the car and started screaming. I wondered what had happened. Thankfully, she could now tell us.

"What's going on?" Lindsey queried Emily the next day.

I am having screaming fits because my best is not enough. I will not be able to ever be seen as an intelligent person.

"So, you went to a party . . . ?"

I don't want to go to parties like that ever again. I hate getting so worked up.

Tom and I left the room to give the girls privacy. Soon, though, Lindsey called us back in.

"I asked Emily to type again what she just told me."

Emily bent over the iPad. *Can you please come back to my session? I like having you in the room so we can talk.*

I was touched that she wanted to share even the difficult parts with us. Tom and I sat at the dining room table, Emily and Lindsey's new working spot where the iPad could be propped up.

I want to say that my screaming is my only way to get my frustrating feelings to come to the surface.

"I'm sorry the party upset you," I said. "I thought you'd enjoy the social outing."

I am thankful for you wanting me to be social but I think I need a different crowd.

"What about dance or tennis?" I offered.

I am able to enjoy all my activities a lot but too much of the time people act like I am too stupid to be doing anything else. I really want to be the strong silent type but I am just me. Please tell me it gets easier with communication.

"I love sitting across the table and talking to you," I said, feeling my throat tighten. "Do you know that?"

Too often we don't get to talk because I don't have speech. Let's keep working on that.

I left that session with profound hope. Emily wanted to share her life with us in a meaningful and intimate way. Later, we figured out that being with a group of autistic people often made Emily upset because she wanted to be seen as more neurotypical and felt limited by association with that community. Her attitudes about this changed over time, and she has since embraced her autistic friends more fully, but initially, I think, she wanted to break as free from the autism as possible. She'd felt hemmed in by the others at that party, continually reminded by their presence of her own differences.

WHEN THERE WAS no set topic for discussion, Lindsey read articles and engaged Emily in questions. More often, though,

Emily now directed the conversations. Some of her messages concerned daily human interactions, how she was feeling on a given day, or telling Lindsey what her weekend had been like. One day, Emily let us know she didn't care for the voice on her iPad.

Let's talk about something Apple could do to help someone like me by not making the iPad sound so robotic.

To know the voice did not give her pleasure was, for us, monumental. For two and a half decades we'd had to guess what Emily liked and didn't like. Sometimes her refusal to do something appeared like straight-up obstinance. I remember when she was in preschool and didn't want to eat the Ritz crackers at snack with the other kids. I wanted her to be like all the other kids and eat the crackers. Now that she could communicate, she could add nuance and clarity. It turned out that she simply disliked Ritz crackers. If the school had offered her another kind of cracker, she would have gladly eaten them. At the time, I thought she was just being difficult, that it was her autism I was seeing in that refusal, and it so disheartened me. To learn that she simply hated Ritz crackers made such sense. Likewise, to now find out that, like the crackers, she didn't care for the robotic voice: great. Let's bring on a new voice. We were starting to finally know what our daughter was genuinely thinking and who she was. We found an application with differing voices that would read her words aloud. She found one she liked.

ONE MORNING, LINDSEY asked Emily if she'd had a good night's sleep.

I often go right into a dream where I am a talking person.

The last part of it is always the same. I am ordering food at a totally cool restaurant, everything on the menu. Then I wake up and I'm still very much stuck in a body that does not work that way.

Hearing the iPad speak those words aloud, I felt pinned in place by sadness. We shared a similar grief. Both Tom and I had had the same recurring dream of Emily being able to speak. It was always so vivid. Even my assistant at work had told me how she'd also dreamed of Emily speaking. The reality was that she'd likely never "speak" in the way she did in all our dreams. She could enunciate a few words but much of what she might try to tell us verbally was not understandable, a frustration to all of us. Though this realization of what she'd likely never be able to do was poignant, it didn't diminish how world-shattering her typed words were—for all of us.

AT ONE OF their sessions, Lindsey asked what Emily thought about her leap forward with typing. How had it happened?

I think it just happened directly after that horrible flight home from Ireland. I could not tell anyone about my anxiety about being on that damn plane for so long. It made me realize that something had to change. I knew that you would help me.

This was the first time we really understood. I'd never connected the two events before. Later, Emily wrote a whole essay on that flight, as if it had just occurred, giving us stunning insight into a moment that had left us traumatized and depressed.

Every time she wrote, I felt awed and humbled. We were finally being admitted into the closed-off room that had long been Emily's life. At last the walls that had long kept us separated were coming down and we could know our daughter. And the diction. I wondered how a person goes from making zero sentences over twenty-five years to this kind of writing, so fluid and perceptive.

IN ADDITION TO writing her thoughts, poetry, and prose, Emily also showed us her heart. Gratitude was an element that showed up again and again. One morning, she was having a meltdown when Lindsey arrived. Once Lindsey got her redirected, she asked what had happened.

I am upset because I couldn't talk to Marta. I don't think I ever have.

Marta had been her day-to-day aide since before Emily left the UCLA program, someone she went on regular outings with.

"Would you like to write her a note?" Lindsey asked.

To Marta,

Thank you for being there for me all this time. Makes me truly better to go places with you. The things we do are so important so let's keep being better friends on courage and commitment. Thank you again my dear friend.

Love, Emily.

Emily was not only able to communicate basic wants and needs with us, she was able to let the people she cared about know that they mattered to her. You could see the satisfaction on her face when the iPad read the letter to Marta. Emily's gratitude had been voiced.

17

Initially, Emily typed only with Lindsey. Then she tried with Marta, and though not as smooth, the process still worked. Marta asked her questions, nudged her sleeve, and Emily responded. Soon Lindsey introduced Emily to one of her other clients, Anna, an autistic woman five or six years younger who'd been typing for some time. Lindsey thought it would be fun for the two girls to meet.

Through emails and phone calls with Anna's parents, I arranged to have Anna come to the house for a visit. We hoped the two young women would be able to have a conversation with each other.

Anna is a beautiful young woman with long strawberry blonde hair and huge, round blue eyes. When she came to our door, I was struck by her beauty as well as the noise-canceling headphones she regularly wore to reduce sound disturbances. Emily was eager to meet and converse with Anna; it was really her first time to "talk" with anyone who was even close to being a peer. Lindsey was there to mediate.

Emily first apologized to Anna for being so loud with

her noises—she's always self-conscious about them—then told Anna that she was scared of not being able to live on her own, jumping almost immediately away from small talk and into the profound circumstances the two young ladies shared. When you've spent a quarter of a century not communicating, you don't have time to waste on chitchat. Emily passed her iPad to Anna since it had become clear that Anna's battery wasn't charged and her own device wouldn't turn on.

Anna typed: *I am not sure I could handle being on my own.*

Before the conversation could go much deeper, though, the anxiety that often comes with autism grabbed hold of Anna. She was feeling insecure. *I want my iPad. I do. I am sorry but I'm really anxious without my ipad.*

Emily eased her concerns by sharing her own fears.

I am always anxious without my parents, Emily wrote. *I think I would like to* [try living on my own again] *some other day.*

Emily suggested that she and Anna work together to type *roaring answers to life's questions and break down the stereotype that spills into our autistic being.* From the very moment she could type, Emily focused on changing perceptions about the autistic community, being an activist in her own way. Together, they wrote about misconceptions people harbored about them and how upsetting they were. They commiserated. Before they finished for the day, Emily confided that she wanted *really badly to have good friends. Please come again my new friend.*

It was the first time Emily had had a conversation with a friend.

IN THE DAYS that followed, Emily wrote mantras for herself: *I am in control of my body. I can be calm.* She asked us to print them so she could read them whenever she got too worked up.

AT ONE OF their sessions, Lindsey asked Emily if she could go anywhere in the world, where would she go. Emily was full of ideas and dreams, but the biggest one, the one she wrote about most frequently, was to visit London. We were astounded as she told us details of the city: She pictured Big Ben and the soldiers with enormous hats, she knew about the River Thames, and that tall red buses filled the streets. She was fascinated by Lady Di and knew all about her and her tragic death. We didn't know where all this information had come from. We'd never told her anything about London. She told us she'd learned about it from watching the news; she'd been five at the time that Lady Di died.

I hoped that one day we could plan such a trip. Still, the angst of Ireland was still too fresh in my mind. With her new ability to communicate, though, things might be different. Anything was possible.

AFTER EMILY'S BREAKTHROUGH, Lindsey called her boss, Darlene Hanson, to tell her what had happened. Darlene had been the one to tell us she didn't think Emily would ever type because she had "too much language." Now she was overjoyed by this news.

I made an appointment for the three of us and Lindsey to see Darlene. I wanted her to assess Emily, to see how she and Lindsey were working together in case she had suggestions on how to improve their dynamic. Finally, I wanted her to teach me and Tom how to become a communication partner to Emily. To be able to have a one-on-one conversation with my daughter was a dream; I hardly allowed myself to consider how intimate and precious such an experience would be for me. I was hoping Darlene would hold the key to that dream.

"Well, let's see what you got, Emily," Darlene said, having exchanged hellos and Darlene telling us that her daughter was getting married in a few days. Darlene sat next to Emily and positioned the iPad between them, grasping hold of Emily's elbow. In seconds, the two were talking, Emily's thoughts being read aloud by the app. At first, Darlene typed with Emily; they discussed Emily's desire to type with me and Tom and how much more peaceful she felt now that she could communicate. Darlene tried to teach us what she did so that we could type with her. I went first.

"Read aloud this article about pandas," Darlene instructed me.

I did so.

"Now put your hand on Emily's elbow and ask her some questions."

I followed her instructions. "What colors are pandas?" I tried.

Emily looked flummoxed.

"Ask, maybe, what a panda might like to eat, or how a panda might want to spend its day . . . ?" Darlene prompted.

I tried to come up with interesting questions but panicked. My powers of imagination were so limited. I felt stupid. Whatever inane questions I came up with, Emily simply responded by typing the last word I spoke, nothing more. No flowing, magical sentences like she wrote with Lindsey. No lyricism.

I wanted so badly to be able to type with her; I was frustrated. She could feel that, I'm sure. I don't think my willfulness helped. The more I exerted myself to be a good facilitator, the more agitated and nervous I became. If it was this hard for me, who was neurotypical, I had some tiny inkling of how hard typing must be for Emily.

Darlene took the iPad from me and asked Emily what was happening.

In two seconds, Emily's fingers again danced on the keyboard. *Possible that it's just going to take more practice,* Emily typed.

Tom tried next. He got a bit further. She was able to answer some of his questions, and he was much better about making up interesting questions. Still, her diction was garbled—*Dad it little well coming calm my came*—not the straightforward and expressive answers she usually gave to Lindsey.

The minute Darlene took over again, though, Emily was discerning and clear in her responses.

I think the problem is that we are too emotional with each other. Typing together will eventually take its place but I think it will be a long process.

As we prepared to leave, Emily typed, *Thank you Darlene. I hope the wedding goes well.*

OVER TIME, TOM and I have tried on multiple occasions—with Lindsey, Darlene, and other facilitators—to type with Emily.

Our success has been, and continues to be, very limited. She'll sometimes give us a sentence or two, but they're never the detailed writings she creates with others. We continue to try. She has, however, made strides with many others.

At her next session with Lindsey, Emily expressed her frustrations in trying to type with us and helped us understand.

It's not going as well as I would like with mom and dad. Only seem to get stressed out when we try to type. Maybe offer to try typing more. Doing better to calm each other would have a positive effect. Lots of time in the minutes I am upset I won't want to type but I am sure I will want to talk about it after.

"Parents are just the hardest people for individuals to type with, the emotionality of it," Darlene told me later. "The vulnerability is huge."

Still, I kept trying to plant the seed. "Look," I told Emily. "It would make it so much easier if you could type with us because then we would be able to get all the stuff out of you on a daily basis."

Practicing with mom and dad is the priority, Emily wrote to Lindsey. *Please let's try on Saturday to type with them.*

We tried with Emily again and again, but her ability to type with me and Tom didn't change. She typed with her psychologist, with Darlene, with other FC practitioners, with Anna and other autistic people. Just not with us.

EMILY'S TWENTY-FIFTH BIRTHDAY approached and we threw a small party as we did every year. To those who would be attending, a number of whom were also autistic, she was the same Emily she'd always been. Most didn't know about her breakthrough. Emily decided to tell them. The next time Lindsey came over, she asked to write a letter to share at the party.

> *Dearest friends,*
>
> *Thank you for coming to my party. Knowing each of you just makes my life better in many ways. Many of you are unaware that I have found a new way to communicate through typing. It has truly changed my life in ways I go to lengths to try to understand and the impact of it is greater than I am able to even put into words. I hope with all my heart that very soon each of you will have a chance to get your feelings and thoughts communicated. Thank the people in your lives that help you to be your best self for giving their time. Make sure all the time to do the best you can. Thank you all again for coming and for listening to my story.*

Though she presented herself as so confident and together in that message, like most of us, she was feeling emotions behind the scenes that one wouldn't know just from observing her. The story behind the story came out when Lindsey was over.

I am all emotions today. Maybe something about being a year older makes me think about what I am going to do with my life. I am eventually going to need time in college. Places around the world I want to see and people I meet get feeling anxious about it, the kind of anxious that gets me all worked up.

I think about what I want to study in school. Maybe something in the field of law. I would like to be an advocate for lots of autistic people that have not yet found a voice. Lots of us are trapped inside bodies not connected to our mind. Makes for a very challenging existence. People need the back bone of someone strong to carry the weight of all the people who adopt the wrong idea about autistic people.

Reading her words, particularly those giving us insight into what it's like to be autistic, was astounding. Like having someone who's blind paint you a picture of what their inner vision looks like, what they see. She was using words to tell us what it's like to be nonverbal.

It was hard to fully comprehend what we were seeing. Before this, Emily had never written even one complete sentence, never mind an essay, a poem, a short story, all of which now started to flow from her fingertips.

I SHOWED EMILY'S work to my colleagues at my office. Many of them were thrilled and supportive and freely commented that this confirmed what I had always said about Emily— that she was really intelligent. One of my closer friends re-minded me how Emily, in her younger days, did her math homework while seated at my office desk. "I'll never forget how quickly she tore through her math problems."

Not everyone was on board with it.

Tom and I were hesitant to tell people beyond our imme-diate circle that Emily was communicating and the method-ology being used. I worried that they might not believe us, or might hold the FC controversies against us and Emily.

AS THANKSGIVING APPROACHED, Emily wanted to write a letter to friends and family in what was effectively her public debut as a communicator.

Many of you do not know that I have found a new way to communicate through typing. It has changed my life in ways I go to lengths to understand and its impact is greater than I am able to put into words. I would like my dear friends and loving parents to know this Thanksgiving what I am grateful for. I must begin with my amazing mom. She has never treated me as a burden but only as smart and capable. For her I am truly grateful and I am honored to be her only daughter. My father must come next. I am really the luckiest to call such a kind and genuine man my dad.

I sat on the couch next to Tom, reading the message she'd composed with Lindsey, holding back tears.

"Read this," I told him. The message continued.

Something I need you all to hear is this: I am autistic, not brain-dead. Please never again under estimate people like me. We make noises and do peculiar things with our bodies, that is undeniable. However our greatest affliction is that the world sees us as incapable of anything else. Make me proud to be a part of this world by helping me eradicate the misconceptions. Please know that I am thankful for each one of you and that you have taken the time to hear my words.

Let's all enjoy this meal and take the time always to be grateful to each other and go from here with new eyes for people on the autism spectrum.

I put my head on his shoulder and cried. Our daughter has so much to say, so much eloquence that had been silenced for so long.

"It's beautiful," he said, grabbing a tissue himself. "She might like us to post it on Facebook."

I checked with Emily. She liked that idea.

"WHAT'S GOING ON?" Tom's niece Annie, an attorney in Atlanta, contacted us immediately after I posted Emily's message. "How is this happening?" she asked.

I have only a few followers on Facebook and am not very active on social media, so I was surprised to hear from anyone—and so quickly. Over the years Annie had had limited contact with Emily as she lived in the Southeast portion of the US and we rarely visited with her and her family. Now, however, she was insistent. We filled her in, and before we were done talking, Annie was in tears.

She reposted Emily's message on her own Facebook page: "Below is . . . from my cousin, Emily Grodin. She is 25 years old and is autistic, and in all the times I've been with her, we've never had a conversation, I've only heard her say 'hi.' She has recently found her voice, and it's incredible to hear it. Emily, I love you and can't wait to hear what you have to say!"

The number of likes, comments, and shares to Annie's post humbled me. Hundreds of people from across the country, people who didn't know Emily, who would never meet Emily, were weighing in, congratulating her, encouraging her, telling her they looked forward to what she had to say.

For a quarter of a century we'd felt so alone and isolated in parenting and raising Emily, and I'm sure her sense of seclusion and loneliness far exceeded our own. Now it was as if two and a half decades of isolation were evaporating before our eyes. Emily, and by extension Tom and I, were rejoining the world. I hadn't realized how Emily's silence had kept her apart, not only from Tom and me, but from family and friends who wanted to know her. The world was asking to hear from her, wanting to know her. We finally realized that Emily's breakthrough was real.

Thanks to this breakthrough, she was able to tell us more about her experiences, often through poetry.

Emily was happier than we'd ever seen her, full of ideas and plans. The big idea that kept coming up over and over again was to attend college. Santa Monica College (SMC), in particular. I don't know where that specific choice came from other than we listened to NPR in the car occasionally—when Emily would reluctantly let me turn the dial from K-EARTH 101 and their eighties and nineties music to the public news station. KCRW is a National Public Radio member station that broadcasts from Santa Monica College. It was the NPR station we listened to as it came in with the strongest reception. They frequently mentioned on the air that they were located at Santa Monica College. So, she clearly learned about SMC while listening to the radio.

I am so eager to be a college student, she wrote. *I would like to take a course on political science and some thing in creative writing. I want to say thank you mom for believing in my ability to make a mark in this world. Dad you have always been my strongest supporter and I can't say thank you enough. My education links me to the rest of the world.*

"College," Tom said, shaking his head in admiration. We'd struggled to get her through preschool, kindergarten, grade school, then middle school and high school. And now college. We'd climbed so many mountains together.

Now she wanted to climb Everest.

18

Hello fellow students,

My name is Emily Grodin. I am 25 years old and really looking forward to sharing my first college class with all of you. I appreciate the opportunity to introduce myself in an earnest attempt to explain some things you'll undoubtedly notice about me throughout the semester.

In so many ways, I am just like everyone else. I am, however, also very different. I am autistic and might exhibit some unusual behaviors in class from time to time. I will do my best not to be a distraction, but ask for your understanding in advance.

Please know that my most expressive communication requires me to type with the help of a trained communication partner. Despite my ability to speak, my thoughts and feelings may not be best conveyed through speech. I hope this will not discourage any of you from saying hello. I welcome your questions and friendships. Although my responses may be a bit delayed I assure you they are no less heartfelt.

Thank you for your time and let's have a great semester!

Stuck in bumper-to-bumper traffic on the I-405 south, I scowled and worried we'd be late. Everyone else in Los Angeles suddenly needed to be driving in the same direction we were. Next to me in the passenger seat, though, Emily, couldn't stop grinning. Her singsong noises lightened my mood; her exuberance and high energy filled the confined space.

"You're certainly in a good mood," Lindsey offered from the back seat.

"Yes," Emily quipped in her high-pitched, clipped tone. She did a little dance in her seat.

We were en route to Santa Monica College to meet her first-ever college counselor and to have her first-ever conversation about attending college.

After we parked, I realized we'd arrived in plenty of time. We still had to meet up with Marta, who'd be accompanying Emily to her classes. While we looked for the Center for Students with Disabilities and coordinated meeting up with Marta, Lindsey snuck away for a moment.

"Look what I have for you." When Lindsey returned, she offered Emily a bag from the college bookstore. Emily clapped her hands and took the gift, opening it to find a Santa Monica College sweatshirt. She held the sweatshirt to her, her face split with satisfaction.

As we navigated our way through campus, Emily wandered through a field of college students going about their normal day. The joy on her face was unmistakable as she imagined herself among them, her new sweatshirt in hand. She walked taller and held her head higher than I'd ever seen before.

ONCE WE LOCATED Marta, the four of us signed in and seated ourselves in the disability center's waiting room, the buzz of excitement among us electric. While we waited for Emily's appointment, a man with a red-tipped cane, indicating a visual impairment, came in looking for help. Then a woman in a wheelchair. A handful of others also approached the main counter asking for advice or services to address the needs of those with learning disabilities, mental health issues, and cognitive challenges.

"Welcome. How can I help?" The employee behind the counter was full of sunshine for each person who approached. I was immediately impressed. After years of bringing Emily to all sorts of educational institutions and being greeted by people who often saw us as a problem to be dispatched as quickly as possible, to be gotten out of the way, this was encouraging.

"HI, EMILY. MY name's Nathalie." The fifty-something woman who came to greet us invited us into her office. All four of us crowded into the small space. "I'm a special education counselor here at Santa Monica College. What can I do for you?"

I'd called ahead and made the appointment with Nathalie Laille, the faculty coordinator in the disability resources center, explaining Emily's specific circumstances. It was December first, a little more than three months since Emily had started typing and said she was ready to take this big step. Nathalie knew from our earlier conversation that the iPad was how Emily communicated. She waited as

Lindsey handed the tablet to Emily and held her shirtsleeve to prompt her.

Please tell me how to become a student, Emily typed.

I'd worried that Emily might withdraw inside herself at this interview. We'd discussed at home her desire to speak for herself and for us to take a back seat. And now, she was doing it.

"What are you interested in?" Nathalie asked.

I'd like to take a creative writing course.

"The first thing is to take the proficiency test," Nathalie explained.

OK.

Emily knew about the test. Before coming to the appointment, we'd talked about how she'd need to score well to be enrolled in regular classes. The test would take place in a special room with a proctor to verify that answers being entered into the computer were Emily's and not Lindsey's. She wouldn't have any trouble with it.

When we discussed class offerings, Nathalie tried to steer Emily toward more personal enrichment–type classes, electives like music appreciation, classes that wouldn't require the entrance exam. She offered up many choices, as Emily respectfully listened. This is how students with special needs are often encouraged to start easy to see if they are up to the full-on college-level work. Emily remained polite but held her ground.

Learning is so important to me. I would like to take courses in political science, history, and language arts.

"So we'll have to schedule the test first to see where to place you and what classes you can take."

Yes. Ok. I'll take the test as soon as possible.

"Would it be okay if Emily typed a letter to her professors to introduce herself?" Lindsey asked. "She'd like them to know more about her prior to the start of the class. We talked about this at home."

"She could, but maybe it would be best if I sent the email first," Nathalie said.

Please let me type to my professors myself. My independence is very crucial for my future as a college student.

"I think we can arrange that." Nathalie smiled at me and then turned her attention back to Emily. "Do you have other questions?"

Would people ask me to leave if I make noise in class?

"Can you explain what you mean?" Nathalie asked.

Something I do in moments of stress is make noises. Really worried it may be distracting for others.

"Please don't worry about that now," Nathalie said. "We'll take things one step at a time."

We left the campus with Emily clutching her college sweatshirt and beaming as if she'd just won the lottery. She was going to become an actual college student taking a real for-credit undergraduate class. That is, if she could pass the English proficiency exam.

EMILY TOOK THE college English proficiency test a week later.

I am totally happy with my test results. Lindsey I am so ready for the next step, she wrote when they got home after the test.

It was no wonder she was pleased. She'd scored 97 percent. All those times when I kept insisting she was smart, I'd always worried I might be projecting my wishes onto her. Now there was no question: 97 percent spoke volumes.

EMILY AND LINDSEY sat together at the dining room table, the iPad before them a week or so later. Tom was in the room, wanting to hear Emily's thoughts on the world and her place in it. Lindsey suggested that perhaps Emily would like to write a poem.

"Do you need help getting started?" Lindsey asked.

Emily's "no" was loud and clear. Immediately, she began to write.

In the world of autism, this was a pretty radical act. Many consider autistics to be highly literal, and therefore, locked out of the realm of poetry, replete as it is with metaphor and imaginative leaps. Tom was shocked when poetry emerged almost like magic on the iPad.

PEOPLE.

People stare.
People judge.
They think they know the truth, but they do not.
People listen.
People scorn.
Like minds unfold in loudly raucous voices that burn
People take.
People open.
Those together knowingly remain with greatness unwound and
Broken.
People be wary.
People gather the one who you never thought ever.
I will not go silent in spite of ignorance.
People hear me.
People change.

"I couldn't stop staring as her words jumped off the screen," Tom said. "Not only could Emily communicate, she was a poet."

We'd never read much poetry to her. We'd made sure she was exposed to all the arts—music, theater, visual arts, performing arts, dance, improv, novels, you name it—but poetry? It had never really been our thing. And yet, poetry became her milieu.

Tom was especially pleased. "My father, Eddie, though he was a highly regarded lawyer, writing was his first love. Whenever I see Emily put out these pieces, I wish he was here to see it with me. He would go crazy. Writing was his passion. He would be so proud of her."

WITH THE RESULTS from her entrance exam in place, Emily enrolled in English 1 at Santa Monica College with Mr. Pacchioli as the instructor, a class that would begin in February 2017. Just prior to the start of class, Emily (with Lindsey's tugs on her sleeve) wrote the following email.

Hello Mr Pacchioli,

My name is Emily Grodin and I am enrolled in your English 1, section 1910. Per the advice of my counselor Natalie I am writing to introduce myself and tell you about what it might be like to have me in your class.

I should tell you that I am autistic although I sincerely hope that you will choose to not define me by my diagnosis. The most important thing for you to know about me is how I communicate. I type my thoughts on an IPad with the help of a trained communication partner.

Having this experienced individual is a crucial part of my being able to express myself. I will be attending class with my friend Marta who has been with me for years. She knows me very well but she is still learning to type with me. I may not be able to participate fully in class discussion or answer questions unless materials are provided ahead of time to allow me the chance to type a response before coming to class. Please send me as much information as you can ahead of time and I will do my best to be as included as my classmates.

I would be grateful for a seat near an exit in case I need to excuse myself. Sometimes I make noises and movement with my body that may seem strange or disturbing to others. Please know that I am doing my best not to disrupt the class and may step outside to get myself regulated.

I appreciate your time and invite any questions you may have. In an effort to increase acceptance of people like me I would be so thankful if you would allow me the opportunity to introduce myself to the rest of the class. I will prepare something ahead of time to play on my device.

Thank you again for your time. I look forward to meeting you and taking your class.

With warm regards,
Emily Grodin

Marta would accompany Emily to her classes as Lindsey had other clients scheduled during that time. Marta would take notes for Emily and, if a meltdown occurred, whisk her out of the classroom before the meltdown became disruptive.

She would also facilitate Emily's contribution to the class if called upon to answer a question.

EMILY WAS UP and dressed early that first day, so excited to start. It was February 2017. She'd never fought me about attending school, had always enjoyed it, but this exuberance and anticipation were new. Not only was she going to attend school, she was going to college and taking a class of her choosing. For the first time, she was demonstrating autonomy in her life, directing what she wanted and going after it. We discussed this before she left home.

Today opens a new world of doors for me. I am fully ready to tackle the college scene.

"Are you worried about anything?"

Please can we look at some more ways to help me not to have a meltdown at school?

We went over her list of strategies, including breathing, stepping outside if she needed to compose herself, reminding herself that she was in control of her body, and visualizing placing her noises in a wooden box.

I want to go mom. Makes me so thrilled to be finally to this day. I cant wait to show everyone that I can do this. Can't believe I'm really a college student! This is a huge milestone and I'm not going to take it for granted.

PRIOR TO THIS day, Emily had composed a letter to her fellow students to answer their questions about her and to put them at ease.

Marta later recounted the scene for me. After taking roll and going over the class syllabus, Mr. Pacchioli invited Emily to present the letter she'd written for her classmates. Marta and Emily stood up and made their way to the front of the room. Marta pressed the iPad button to read Emily's missive. *Hello fellow students . . .*

When the iPad grew quiet, just about every kid in the classroom had tears in their eyes. They wanted Emily in the class and they let her know it, clapping to show their encouragement. Emily, Marta reported, beamed.

19

I want to talk about my personal life by myself. I mean alone without a boyfriend. I'm afraid I'll never have someone. Because I need special consideration from a guy. I am curious about Nik's girlfriend because I wonder what he likes in a girl. I think other girls offer more than me to a man. I don't speak with my mouth. I also make noises growl yell hit scratch and flip my fingers. I don't want anyone but my parents to see this. And they should not feel sorry for me. I know I need to meet a man who is not already taken. I have not met that guy yet.

Where do I meet someone? I don't have many ideas. Dances, parties, school. I know people meet people online. What should I do online? I want someone to know I am smart. I am funny and have a good sense of humor. I like many things and am interested in politics religion and most things people have to talk about. I am unique in that I type to talk. That is unique and fantastic. I am glad others agree. I feel good that people see me as special and coming out and transforming into a real participant in life. It was harder before.

I was nervous as we entered the small student-gathering hall at Los Angeles Valley College, but also excited. It was lunchtime and the Black Scholars Club was setting up for the occasional poetry reading they hosted. One young man stacked boxes of pizza on a table, the scent of pepperoni and green peppers wafting our way. A young woman arranged cans of soda, laughing and teasing a classmate. Others set chairs around the large round tables filling the room. The center area, framed by a fireplace, would be the makeshift stage.

The day was overcast and Emily had dressed in a soft yellow cowl-neck sweater that set off her dark hair. Her eyes were bright and attentive behind the geeky-cool black-framed glasses she'd chosen. Snug jeans and Converse All-Stars completed the look of an average SoCal college student. She hung with us in the back of the room, but was seriously eyeing the pizza.

Emily had previously attended a few of the group's poetry readings and had been inspired by what she'd seen. Today, though, she was not going to be just another audience member. She was an emerging poet about to give her first-ever public reading.

It had been a long and oftentimes exhilarating road to get here.

IN THE TWO years since she began to communicate, Emily had taken a handful of college classes, first at Santa Monica College and then at Los Angeles Valley College, including English 1 and 2, African American literature, history, poetry, and psychology. With Marta or Lindsey at her side to take notes and to help her type if the professor asked her a question, she was able to attend and finish all the work. She spent hours each day completing assigned essays and studying for tests. She took her schoolwork seriously.

With every single class she took, there was the inevitable meltdown during one of the first sessions. When that happened, Lindsey or Marta whisked Emily out of the room and brought her home. Once calmed, she was able to tell us how her excitement had overflowed its banks, causing the commotion. After that initial breakdown, though, she was able to be present, to listen and absorb, and refrain from making noises. It was like she needed to get that one outburst out of the way in order to settle down and move forward. I attended the occasional class with her and was amazed to see how quiet, attentive, and studious she was when engaged. It was like encountering a different Emily.

She became an outstanding student. One day, Lindsey was in the process of reviewing her English class notes with her for an upcoming exam. As Lindsey tried to go over the details with Emily, she discovered that Emily didn't need to see, read, or be reminded of the material the professor had covered. Emily could almost recount the professor's lectures verbatim; her memory and attentiveness were that sharp.

Whenever tests were assigned, Emily went to the college's testing center to complete them with Lindsey as her facilitator. The proctors kept a keen eye to make sure Emily was the one taking the test. Believe me, Emily would not have tried to cheat. She wanted to prove something—to us, to herself, to the world. She was smart and wanted to show us.

Her GPA was outstanding. Emily was thriving, even making dinners for Tom and me.

TUESDAY NIGHT DINNER

To anyone else it would be just a Tuesday. To people like me it's the opportunity to give back just a little to the ones who have given me everything.

Flipping through the pages, I can't help but wonder if Martha Stewart cooks the thousands of recipes filling her many cookbooks or if there is a team of people behind her creating and testing each one. There is no way the maven of doing-everything-better-then-your-average-housewife does everyone on her own. I am no Martha Stewart. Nonetheless, it's my night to cook tonight so here goes.

Tonight's menu is shepherd's pie and salad. Looking through the recipe book of family favorites I turn to the page and begin to convert the list of ingredients into a shopping list. Damnit, my handwriting looks like a toddler's scribbles! Maybe I'll just take the recipe. I really don't even like shepherd's pie. I would never eat anything but cake and pasta if I could get away with it. My mother's mission to incorporate variety into my diet, coupled with an ever-present concern for my independence, is what brings us to this moment. To Tuesday night dinner by yours truly.

Maybe I'm playing with the idea of being truly independent. Living every day as someone seen as incapable of being alone is a very interesting thing. There is always someone close-by in case I lose it. That does happen. I do on occasion lose control and become powerless against a storm of anxiety and fear. I wait for it to pass and begin to assess the damage.

Perhaps learning to cook can help me in some ways. Maybe just being able to control myself enough to contribute something, maybe that's enough. I do enjoy it. I really find it makes me feel a certain sense of accomplishment.

Looking through the aisles in the maze that is the grocery store I often struggle to focus. My mind is mostly lost in having to take in massive amounts of input through my over-sensitive sensory system. Input that to anyone might go completely unnoticed might at any moment send me spinning. Lights flickering. Shoes are all different and each make particular sounds on every different floor. I can hear everything. In my mind the sounds swirl like a tornado. I am caught in the middle, powerless. Making my way through the chaos to find what I need. My movements are frantic. Task must be completed. That's the way my mind works: like millions of tiny boxes waiting to be checked off. If only I could check them off more easily. I get stuck waiting for a cue, some kind of prompt to move, to go through the motions. I know what I need to do yet I'm frozen in anticipation of someone's voice or gesture to trigger my action. I'd like to someday let that go. I finally get what I need from the store and head home.

Potatoes, I have to boil them. Carrots and onions need to be sliced. Using a knife, I must be collected, in control. I am finding the peace to slow down, even if for only long enough to chop a carrot or two. Maybe my parents can see that it's possible, that maybe soon I may need them just a little less. I know they need that. To be needed less means they have a chance to feel like other parents do when their children become more self-sufficient, even leave home. Right now it's just dinner, and right now, that's enough.

The smells waft through the house and hearing my dad's

anticipation makes me feel proud of what I'm doing. Not because I'm a woman and feel it is my job to be in the kitchen cooking for the sake of a man. It's because I am an autistic adult and it feels damn good to sit down to enjoy a meal that I prepared with the two people who have spent my entire twenty-eight years taking my best interest to heart. Let me be capable of filling their bellies tonight. Let me be the one to give this time.

When Lindsey first announced she was moving away from the Los Angeles area in July 2017, we'd made the decision to transfer Emily from Santa Monica College to Los Angeles Valley College. It was closer to home and would make hiring a communication facilitator easier. Emily still had Marta who could type with her and accompany her to classes, but we were hoping to find another who could help with homework and studying.

Lindsey suggested Stephanie, a young woman who'd once been Lindsey's roommate; she'd learned how to facilitate communication directly from Lindsey herself. Stephanie, like Lindsey, was bright and enthusiastic, someone who could joke with Emily and cajole her. Now Emily attended classes with either Stephanie or Marta, and on the weekends, a young screenwriter named Nik came to work with her on her creative writing. Nik was a handsome young man of Indian extraction who'd learned to be an FC facilitator.

It was so funny to see Emily and Nik working together. Emily would often ask him about his love life—she was gathering intel on how relationships among twenty-somethings worked. She reported back to Stephanie after Nik left.

She also made up fictional stories of her own experiences

that she passed off to Nik as real. She came up with an elaborate story about how Stephanie had a crush on Nik and was interested in a relationship. This went on for several sessions and I was sure she'd eventually tell him it was a prank. When it became clear she had no intention of letting up, I ended it. There were other stories, too, including her insistence that she regularly watched TV shows he'd either been a writer for or had intimate familiarity with—none of it was true. In addition to being a poet, she was becoming an imaginative writer of fiction.

I don't know if he caught on that she was messing with him. To be honest, I think she had a crush on him. She was spreading her wings, learning how romantic relationships between people her own age worked by asking him questions, and testing him with her stories. She also worked diligently on her poetry.

IT WAS NOVEMBER 2018. Nik was the communication partner who was to join us this day, for her first ever poetry reading. Among the extracurricular activities she'd learned about since coming to Los Angeles Valley College was this poetry event sponsored by the Black Scholars program. I had called the coordinator in advance. "Would it be okay if Emily participated?" I'd explained Emily's limitations and the fact that she was not Black. I was assured she would be most welcome.

The previous Sunday when Nik had been over, I'd suggested he might like to accompany her and be her reader. He'd been enthusiastic. "Want to do it, Em?" he asked.

"Yes." Her clipped assent was full of zeal.

"I can stand up there and introduce you," Nik suggested.

"I'll be your voice for you, reading the work so the iPad doesn't have to. Everyone will know the words are all yours. What do you say?"

"Yes," she said.

Now, though, I wasn't sure if Emily was going to go through with it. She was looking a little scared and overwhelmed. When Nik joined us, though, the two of them made their way to the pizza table and grabbed a slice. If she was downing pizza, I might be wrong. Maybe she was just fine with this entry into the poetry world.

Soon the room quieted down and the emcee asked everyone to please take their seats. I was in the back with Marta, my camera phone at the ready. I wanted to capture this moment on video. First one, then another student got up to read their poetry to polite applause. I looked over to where Nik and Emily were seated to see if I could tell by her posture if the plans to read were a go. It seemed like they were.

The emcee stood after the third reader and leaned into the mic. "We have a student with us today who's come to see us quite a few times and has just decided to share with us. This is what this is about, folks, us getting out of ourselves, sharing ourselves. So she's going to come up with one of her friends."

Nik and Emily took the stage.

"This is Emily," Nik said to the group of thirty or so scholars of color ringing the stage. "What I'm going to read is *her* work. I'm just helping her out here."

Before he started to read, though, he told the gathered students a bit about Emily, explaining that she was a twenty-six-year-old college student. "Like a lot of you, she is into books, politics, TV, and movies, pretty much like any other woman her age."

The reason Nik was up there, he told them, was that she was autistic. "It's not *what* she is, it's not *who* she is, it's just part of her life," he explained.

"I know a lot of you can relate to this. It's not exactly the same as race, but being brown is not *what* I am," Nik said, slotting himself comfortably into this room filled with other people of color. "It's not *who* I am but it's definitely a part of my life, and I wouldn't change that. Autism, on a certain level, is much the same."

Nik explained a bit about Emily's struggles. "We all have those days when we're so hungry, we're so thirsty or caffeinated or distracted or tired that we can't focus on what we want to focus on. We can't even think straight. So it's like two brains: one that's hungry and thirsty and distracted by everything, and your usual brain, the one you use every day."

He asked the group to imagine that conflict, every day, all the time. People in the audience nodded.

"That's what Emily and others have said that autism is like. On top of it, their bodies don't listen to either brain. Think of all that happening at every given moment in your day, and everyone looks at you and they don't understand and think that you don't understand, when actually you understand at a much deeper level than they could because you're stuck with it. That's what a lot of being autistic is and Em has described it for me."

Emily stood next to him, looking a little shy but mostly comfortable, nodding a tiny bit in response to Nik's words.

With that, he read her poetry.

When Emily's portion of the reading finished, applause filled the room. Almost everyone there was a student of color. And here was Emily, as white and privileged—in the traditional sense—as they come. Still, there was a bond, an understanding between the other students and Emily. They'd each struggled to prove themselves, had overcome prejudices and biases that had nothing to do with who they were as individuals. They'd found a way to rise above those obstacles. They all knew, Emily and the Black students alike, that tomorrow the same obstacles would be waiting for them. In this lunchtime poetry reading, though, for this little pizza-fueled time together, they'd found a way to transcend those limitations and prejudices. They'd found a way to connect and empathize with each other.

20

T. S. Eliot once famously wrote in his poem "Little Gidding":

> We shall not cease from exploration
> And the end of all our exploring
> Will be to arrive where we started
> And know the place for the first time.

Thanks to Emily, Tom and I were learning more about poetry, a language we'd never really spoken as attorneys. Poetry, meanwhile, was teaching us more about our daughter and our lives together. These lines from Eliot became particularly apropos as we planned what I'd sworn I'd never do: take another trip to Europe with Emily.

She'd long talked with wonder and excitement about London, and I'd often wistfully wanted to show her Paris, a city where Tom and I had spent considerable time. Maybe this time, we'd come to know Europe and our daughter as if for the first time.

I booked flights via Air France and arranged for Stephanie to join us midway through the trip, when we were still in

Paris, before we continued on to London. That way, Emily could type freely and capture her thoughts as they occurred when Stephanie was around, but also, Tom and I could savor some alone time with Emily.

The flight over was easy. I'd downloaded videos onto Emily's iPad and that kept her occupied. Once we landed, though, the heat was oppressive. Within a day the mercury would rise to 110 degrees.

After we landed and checked into the hotel, we went out for a walk to see Galeries Lafayette, the fancy department store in Paris with its rooftop gardens. Late afternoon began to morph into early evening. Though she was tired, as were Tom and I, Emily took in the experience with open arms. Unlike Ireland, where she'd basically put up with whatever site we dragged her to, Emily was engaged and present now. At the rooftop gardens, Emily stood at the edge taking in the City of Lights spread out beneath her, her face awash in joy. A look of awe and contentment suffused her. I took a mental picture to treasure later: here was my daughter, absorbing Paris, happy to be abroad.

A day or so later we took Emily to the rue Mouffetard, inspired by the words of food writer Ruth Reichl: "Walking down the rue Mouffetard in the early Paris morning is a completely sensual experience. This time of year the street is perfumed with strawberries and the fat white asparagus are everywhere, poking up with a curiously aggressive air. Meanwhile the cauliflower curl shyly into their protective green leaves, as if reluctant to emerge and face the sassy herbs in their bold bunches."*

---

* http://ruthreichl.com/2012/05/notes-from-paris-and-london.html/

I wanted to share that experience with Emily.

Though the inspiring passage I'd treasured mentioned early morning as the time to visit, I'm afraid we arrived a bit too early. French "early" was clearly not the same as the American version. We arrived around nine and the rue wasn't going to fully come awake, we learned, until ten. Still, we sauntered the region's cobblestoned streets, most of the shops not yet open. Tea shops and sweetshops and just about every type of food could be found there. At one point I hung back a bit and watched my daughter make her way down this little French passageway. She was just so curious about everything she saw. Emily was absorbed in the world and this treasure it presented to her. As I watched her stroll, Emily kind of took charge, leading the way, enthusiasm in her step. She wore a cute little dress and the hem of it swung side to side as she walked. You could almost call her stride a swagger. She was the Pied Piper, leading Tom and me through the streets of Paris.

Without Stephanie on hand we couldn't ask her to tell us in detail how she was feeling and what she wanted, still her countenance said it all. She was ecstatic, happy, grinning all the time, and so very easy to be with.

Of course, throughout the trip Tom and I continued to be wary, wondering what might come to pass that we were not expecting. How could we not worry? There is not a day when we do not hold our breath; that's just our reality. It's not that we don't trust Emily to do the right thing, we just know that her disability is still an issue—although increasingly it has not been, or she's been easier to talk down when it is. We still looked at each other and looked for signs. We still asked each other, "Is Emily okay?" We were always mindful.

Now, though, in this one moment on rue Mouffetard, I took the joyful moment for what it was. A chance for us to be together as a family, to be relatively carefree, to be abroad and to be happy.

Stephanie arrived a few days later and we all went to the Eiffel Tower. There was a lot of confusion around which elevator to take, and we were kind of crammed in the one we'd found when someone announced, "This elevator is not working."

I was the first person to hear that announcement and the nearest to the elevator door.

"Come on, let's go." I tugged at Emily and Stephanie. We tore off across the landing to another elevator, Emily laughing. Tom decided the cramped elevator conditions were not for him, so he stayed behind while Stephanie, Emily, and I boarded another elevator and got the best viewing spots possible.

After, we went across the river to the Right Bank to get a picture of Stephanie and Emily in front of the Eiffel Tower from the perspective of the Trocadero. You have to be that far away if you want the whole tower to show up in the picture. I'd brought the girls red berets and bright red lipstick for this moment. They glowed and laughed and it was all I'd dreamed of.

After the Eiffel Tower, I asked Stephanie to take out the iPad. "Let's see what Emily has to say."

Emily let us know that she didn't want to write in that moment, that she preferred to simply soak up the experiences while they were happening. Later she typed that she was processing everything and wanted to figure it out.

ON ONE OF our last days in Paris, we returned to the Champs de Mars area on the Left Bank, to wander through the lovely tree-lined streets. Stephanie had not yet seen the Champs-Élysées, a must for a first-time visit to Paris. We were aware that the Tour de France was coming through later that afternoon, around four. We'd be out of there in plenty of time to avoid the street closure issues, or so I thought.

We walked across the river and wandered among the crowds lined up on the Champs-Élysées who were excited to watch the last leg of the Tour de France. When we'd had enough and wanted to return to our hotel, which was located on the north side of the Champs-Élysées, we realized all the crosswalks back to the north had been closed in anticipation of the arrival of bikers. We couldn't figure out how to get to the hotel. First, we tried a taxi that drove every which way but didn't get us any closer. The taxi driver kept traversing the bridges on the Seine. It was driving us all crazy. After a forty-five-euro fare, we ended his misery and ours by getting out on the Left Bank, at the Pont Neuf. And at that point, Stephanie pulled out her cell phone and she and Emily consulted each other. Then the girls took over and mapped our walk back to the hotel.

"Follow us," Stephanie said as she and Emily took off like bullets. The only reason we could keep up with them was because Emily's mane of hair kept bouncing ahead of us, showing us the way. Every time Tom and I thought we knew the direction we should be heading in, it turned out we were completely wrong.

By then, thankfully, the heat wave had broken so we weren't dripping wet. Together, Emily and Stephanie got us back to the hotel, safe and sound.

LONDON VIA THE Chunnel was next. There were a lot of people on the train and I explained to her where we were.

"Emily, we're under the water." Emily was excited about this next step in our adventure and taking it all in.

"No, we're not," Tom said. "We're not there yet."

The lights were dim and I was pretty sure we were beneath the channel and I said so again, repeating myself.

"We're not," he countered.

Then the light in the train suddenly got brighter. "Oh, I guess we *were* under the water," he conceded. We all laughed.

Stephanie carried with her a pair of Bose sound-canceling headphones she'd borrowed from her boyfriend. When she saw that the sounds of the train and all the people were agitating Emily, she held them out to her.

"Emily, you've *got* to listen. It's so quiet."

Emily shook her head. I'd tried for years to get her to use headphones to soften the cacophony of the world. She always turned me away. This time, though she initially protested, she allowed Stephanie to snug the headphones on her. As soon as the sounds were muffled, the noise of daily life softened a bit, and Emily's face cracked open. Her eyes almost popped out of her head. It was like she was in another world, a world made more comfortable just for her.

LONDON WAS A jewel of an experience for Emily, from start to finish. We saw and did everything she wanted: Big Ben (though it was covered up for restoration), the River Thames, the Tower of London, Westminster Abbey, Buckingham Palace—she was particularly taken with the state rooms there, and surprised by how modern everything was.

Every morning at the hotel buffet breakfast, Emily went to town. Bacon, eggs, croissants, yogurt, you name it. The chefs somehow managed to pile fried eggs one on top of another, so that guests could remove an egg or two to put on their plate. Watching Emily struggle with the slippery eggs, and laughing at herself trying serve them, was delightful. She was having fun, taking things easily, not stressed at all.

WE HAD TICKETS to see a matinee performance of *Come from Away* at the Phoenix Theatre in the West End. That morning found us at the Churchill War Rooms. After spending considerable time engrossed in the exhibit, I realized we had some time before the theater. Westminster Abbey was nearby. We might just have time to fit it in.

"My young adult daughter is disabled," I said to the person at the information desk. The admission line was very long. We'd never make it. "Is there any way we could be permitted to go to the front of the line?"

"Do you have proof of disability?" he asked. I don't usually use Emily's disability to ask for special treatment and now I felt bad that I couldn't prove anything.

"No. We're from California. She has autism."

"Oh. Okay. No problem. Go over there." Thanks to that kindness, we got in in record time, which was a good thing because Westminster Abbey was one of Emily's favorite places on that trip. She later told us she wished we'd had more time there. And more time to eat pub food.

Of all the sights we visited, churches like the Abbey were her favorite. She loved to sit in a church and grow still and quiet. She looked around and took it all in. The coolness, the peacefulness. It's funny: she loved churches the way she did *not* love synagogues. First of all, you can walk freely into a church. These days, you can't do that with synagogues anymore. They've become armed encampments. Whenever we travel, we find Emily drawn to churches. The same was true in London. The art, the vastness of the space—they tend to be very tall. Emily sat in church after church, in awe, in a kind of prayerful or mindful mood, at peace.

Everything about this trip was the opposite of the chaos of Ireland. Communication had changed the experience in the ways I'd long hoped. While Ireland had been my "hoped for" trip to expose Emily to a world I had experienced as a child, it had failed to live up to my dream. This European adventure, by contrast, was everything and more.

We saw in intimate, daily detail how Emily had changed and we appreciated how much better we could now relate to her. She was so thoroughly engaged in every aspect of the trip, albeit cautious in her commentary, waiting to express herself at the right moment. It is impossible to express the gratitude that Tom and I felt at seeing her so absorbed, loving every minute of the experience we had so carefully planned. The failings of the Ireland trip faded into memory, so overwhelmed were we by the sheer joy we experienced in Paris and London.

THE DISTANT SELF

"Doesn't it all seem so distant? As if a different life lived?"
I ask myself in response to her question.
Her question of something so present,
So grand in my happenings,
But today in this moment which feels so far away.
Perhaps it's the thousands of miles which span between myself
*   and the mind that writes tirelessly of life and the events that*
*   have led to this very second.*
It all seems so very distant.

Maybe it's the oceans and channels and state lines that separate me from myself in a different time and space.

I heard her question, know what she refers to, understand that it's my turn to speak.

But oh, how distant it all seems.

A life that exists on a different continent, both in truth and in feeling.

I reach for it, but my fingertips fall so short of that for which I try to grasp.

The question rings in my head, unanswered and unattended.

For I fail to see how a life so full, so rich, so pristine can feel and seem

So very distant from me.

I feel her hand at my shoulder, a gentle pull back to reality.

She smiles, patiently awaiting the response that I don't currently possess.

And all that I can manage,

All I can express,

"Doesn't it all seem so distant?

As if a different life lived?"

Epilogue

Because I write with such clarity, the world wonders why I cannot speak as such. Where I'm from words are celebrated and shared with one another. A book is read at each days end to experience the power of language together. Their messages are discovered in the imaginations that listen. But they still inquire about how I know the things I know.

If I said that differences are accepted and quirks are what make a person human, that there is no trait too odd or too strange or too difficult, would the world wonder how I have been taught to find beauty in myself? How I have learned to find peace in my own experience?

Where I'm from the smells of a home cooked meal is embedded in my nostril. My plate is always full and overflows with unspoken affection. A full table that surrounds me in the comfort of a shared meal and the comfort of my protectors.

Where I'm from Hebrew is heard in foreign and throaty tones. To me it is mostly unknown but a reminder of my roots. Heritage is an excuse to partake in nostalgic traditions and pass plates from one to the next. My blood tells me to be proud in the memories of generations gone.

Where I'm from it is dire to stand up for yourself and defend those in need. To march and to advocate is not a choice, it is crucial and a responsibility. It is okay to change the narrative. It is okay to rewrite the definition if it is false or loose or misleading.

Where I'm from there are sounds that travel through the body and lights that feel like hot beams on my skin. Words like 'stimming' and 'behavior' and 'meltdown' are tossed around like they aren't used to define me. But luckily where I'm from a person can separate themselves from stereotypes and common beliefs.

After our joyful European adventure, daily life continued, and though Emily could now communicate via the iPad with us and the people around her, and her world had opened up in a huge way, so much was still as it always had been—the rest of society ready to persecute those who are different, sometimes harshly.

Her creative writing class was getting ready to end and a classmate used the final assignment to ridicule and mock Emily. Each person was to present a story to the class. One young man wrote about an autistic friend and how the narrator of the story decides it's time to get the autistic boy high via pot brownies. The friend then uses the occasion to tell the autistic boy all the ways he is not normal and not okay, detailing how the traits the narrator doesn't like are all the boy's own fault. By the end of the story, the narrator says he hates his friend and calls him "you autistic fuck." All this, read aloud in class while Emily sat there.

Of course she was upset by this story and she wrote to the professor.

I am trying to understand fully the words I heard in Michael's story yesterday. The story was blatantly offensive and distasteful and I am disappointed greatly in my peer. I have the desire to advocate for my community where they cannot advocate for themselves . . . I believe that words are powerful, stories can be powerful, and to use them in the way that he did is to contribute to the misconceptions and non-acceptance of autism.

Emily and the professor came up with a way to address the issue via Emily's own presentation on the power of words. Together, they decided they'd "teach those who are less compassionate."

I wondered if that presentation changed this young man's anger and venom toward people who are neurodivergent. I don't know.

I *do* know that the experience pained Emily greatly and yet she rose to the occasion with grace and dignity. I wish I could wipe out the stigma associated with autism. In Emily's lifetime that may come to pass, but not likely in mine.

NOT LONG AGO, Tom and I were arguing about something fairly minor, having a disagreement over a contractor we'd hired whose work I found to be unacceptable. I was planning to fire the person but Tom didn't want me to. I could not let the issue go, and as with many seemingly minor matters, I continued to press the matter until Tom ultimately had enough and he pushed back. Soon, the sparks started to fly.

This dispute devolved into a critique of our marriage, and suddenly, instead of arguing over the contractor, we were talking about our partnership. Arguing, really, about our relationship.

As a younger couple, we'd both been frustrated when we realized that Emily's needs and our responsibility to her was putting us on a life trajectory different from almost everyone else we knew. We'd gone into parenthood with certain expectations. Based on our own upbringings, our educational and professional accomplishments, we'd assumed our child would attend a private school, that we would expand our network of friends through her, that she would have friends who came over to play and later hang out with as they grew. Her friends and their families would become our friends, and so our circle would grow and grow. We also expected to have more children.

None of that happened. Our circle did not grow, and we did not have more children. That decision had been agonizing. We'd been waiting for Emily to become verbal to consider a second child. Despite genetic testing, though, we had no way to be sure that lightning wouldn't strike twice. We knew we didn't have the bandwidth for a second child with autism. We had been older parents when Emily was born and taking care of her had stretched us to our limits. Adding to that sadness, we found the boundaries of our world had closed in on us. Even those families with special needs children we came to know were not very social—ourselves included—because the unpredictable behavioral challenges of our kids always had us on edge. We operated in a very small universe, focused on Emily and struggling to sort out her needs. I can't speak for other families, but that is what happened for us. We each had our work life and connections with colleagues that, fortunately, provided some diversion from the concerns we faced at home.

That we'd had a limited social life was probably the biggest strain on our marriage. With so little feedback from anyone who could understand our challenges, we could only bat our issues around with each other. We did not pursue hobbies and other interests outside of raising Emily. Our lives had become incredibly straightforward: work and Emily, which put a lot of pressure on the relationship. And now, it was all coming to a head.

"I'm very unhappy," I said to Tom. "I mean, at this point, of course we're going to stay together, of course we're in it for the long haul. Still, I'm sad and lonely a lot of the time. This is not the partnership I dreamed of."

"Believe me, Valerie," he came back at me, "you're not the only one who's unhappy. This hasn't exactly been what I was signing on for either."

I was a bit shocked to hear him say that. All these years I was sure I was the only one who'd struggled with these feelings. He seemed happy enough within our marriage, content with so much that life had given him. I'd been so caught up with my own wishes and desires, I thought he didn't have any of his own. I believed he was satisfied with the status quo. Now, nearly three decades into our marriage, I was learning that he wasn't.

"You know that I have done everything in my power to make our marriage work," I said defensively. I felt like I had used all my energy and more to make this life of challenges work for all of us. It was a tough balancing act and I had always done what I could to create a happy family life and a lovely home. I wanted my work acknowledged. Tom had made sacrifices, too, but I wasn't in the mood to be generous and acknowledge them.

"Everything and anything I could do for this marriage, I have done," I told him.

Silently, he shook his head, looking down at his hands. "That's not true, Valerie." He wasn't fighting back but acquiescing. That scared me far more than aggressive words would have.

"What do you mean?" I would have preferred a fight to

the kind of quietness and ache I felt in his words. "What have I failed to do? I dare you to come up with a single thing."

He looked up and held my eyes. He wasn't angry. His eyes and body language were calm and yet deeply sad.

"This is the truth, Valerie: Whenever there was a choice to make, you put Emily first. No matter what it was, no matter my thoughts or feelings on the subject, it didn't matter. Emily was always number one." He didn't look away but held my eyes. He wasn't threatening or incensed, but clear.

His words stung. I was preparing my ammunition to bombard him when he reached out and took my hand. "Yes, you put Emily first." He squeezed it and pulled me closer. I wasn't expecting tenderness in that moment.

"And you know what?" he said. "I understand."

I looked at him, this man who'd stood by me and Emily all these years. So many mothers of children with special needs had been left by the child's father at some point, creating fractured homes and lives. Either that, or both parents agreed to have the child spend time away from the family in a specialized residential setting. Though we'd often fought, had not always seen things eye to eye, had struggled with and against each other to get our individual needs met, had seen our hopes and desires as humans greatly limited by our circumstances, Tom and I stayed side by side throughout. We'd both chosen Emily's needs over our own.

"I understand, Valerie. I know why things needed to be this way. It's been hard. There's no question. While I wouldn't change a single thing, I just need you to know this: it's been hard on me, too."

I stood and pulled him up from a seated position, wrapping my arms around him. He was right. I *had* always put Emily first. He'd stayed on board with me—with us—despite that. He was a great man. There could be no deeper form of love than to prize together with someone the brightest light in your life, even when doing so was painful to both of you.

"I love you, Tom." I buried my head in his shoulder. "I love you."

New Year Resolutions
I have so much I aim to accomplish this year. The goals vary a bit from personal to professional. First. I want to write a collection of poems. I already have so many.

A personal goal is to go on a date. That's top of my personal list. It's more fantastical than attainable and I have accepted that. To make that happen, I would have to meet some boys who are on the spectrum, then actually find one I can tolerate. Haha.

Other small goals include trying new foods. I always eat the same things. I want to expand my palate. And I'm hoping to start an exercise regimen.

I want to dance with a boy. I think it can be simple. One song, a slow dance. Like in those high school movies.

I maybe want to sing karaoke. I can't really sing. It's more about putting myself out there.

I also want to learn more about the law. It's what both my parents did and I'm so intrigued by it.

I also want to visit the temple more. I don't really know anything about being Jewish. It's part of me so I want to learn more.

I like this list a lot. It's got some challenges and hard-to-attain goals. But it also has items I can achieve and things to enrich my future.

There were two attitudes shared with us early on in this journey that for a long time I was urged to believe to be true. The first was that we could only access educational programs for Emily once her behaviors were under control. Looking back, I can see that reasoning was faulty. We really never bought into that, although it was promoted by the educational system; we continued to demand that she be fully included in school. Clearly, it was the right decision. As we have come to recognize, even when Emily's behaviors were problematic, she was still learning and growing intellectually. Had we waited until her behaviors were completely in hand, she never would have learned what she did, or had the breakthrough she had.

The second was that of many of the professionals we consulted, that if we pursued any type of augmentative or alternative communication like FC, letter boards, or sign language for Emily, she would never learn to speak. As it turns out, Emily may never "speak" in the traditional sense of the word. However, her use of FC has released her voice, her thoughts, and her opinions, which hitherto had been completely impossible. Do not be afraid to try these modalities.

For all her ability to communicate, though, we still have reason to worry. We don't know what's going to happen to her when Tom and I are gone. We're no closer to a solution than we were before she could type. Yes, communication was key to showing her abilities and breaking down much of her frustration, but it's not the total solution. She still needs a world that understands her and accepts her means of communication. Navigating daily challenges, even those that are routine to many of us, such as ensuring the drugstore fills a prescription correctly or making an in-the-moment decision when an ingredient for a recipe is not available at the market, may well remain challenging, as they are even for many who are not neurodivergent. She will still require support in some form to navigate life's daily tasks. Emily's inability to express herself verbally with the same specificity with which she types will continue to lead to misunderstanding—or not being understood at all.

Looking back from this place where Emily not only can communicate with us but has found personal agency, creativity, and genuine, abiding happiness, though, it's hard to remember the struggles it took to get here. Like a woman forgets the pain of childbirth when she holds her beautiful infant in her arms, I cannot recollect with complete immediacy the struggles, frustrations, and anger that composed our lives until August 6, 2016, when our world changed.

When Emily first wrote on the iPad and we took her to be seen by her neurologist, the doctor proclaimed Emily's typing "a miracle." We heartily agreed and hoped that it would make a huge difference in her life. It has. Yet we both still hope for another miracle. Dare we be so greedy?

"Am I crazy?" Tom asked me recently. "I still haven't given up hope."

WE'D LOVE FOR Emily to be able to express herself verbally. We're not there yet and we may never get there. For now, though, she keeps moving toward a life of increasing independence. One day, we'd like to see her make decisions on her own about her life, break free from other people guiding her choices, and fully experience her own agency and self-determination.

"Could she ever live independently?" Tom asked rhetorically. "I have to be realistic. I'm concerned about her safety. I don't want her to be taken advantage of, or put in a situation she can't handle. She's not an initiator. That may be why she doesn't pick up an iPad and start typing on her own. Maybe part of it is just her disability. Whatever our expectations for her, they're all marked with an asterisk. What does it mean for someone who has her issues?"

We'd both like her to experience the breadth of human interaction, to have life experiences like going to bars with friends, taking trips with girlfriends, falling in love, expanding her relationships, unbridled by and less dependent on others—and on us.

After the iPad breakthrough, we have come to believe in miracles.

Now we fervently hope there are more to come.

If you had asked me ten years ago where I saw myself in five, I probably wouldn't have answered. If you had asked me five years ago where I saw myself in two, I probably wouldn't even have a guess. And if you asked me two years ago where I saw my future taking me, I probably couldn't have anticipated the things I would do. But ask me today where I see myself tomorrow, in two years, even in ten.

Well, let me tell you. Every day is an opportunity for betterment, for growth. Every year is a chance for bittersweet reflection. Every time that someone imposes the question of a future you don't know yet is a moment for self-fulfilling prophecies to be birthed and unnecessary baggage shed.

I once dreaded the question, feared the lack of wholeness that the years to come would deliver at my doorstep. But now I know, truly understand, the importance of such a question and the emotions it stirs in the individual who is expected to answer, expected to know. At last, that this the effect of such a question for the person on the receiving end, a not-so-subtle way of asking "What the hell are you doing with your life?"

Nobody knows, none of us can fathom the grand possibilities, the trauma that can so suddenly alter your world in a flashing second, the relationships of family and friends and mentors that can blossom overnight, or die just as quickly. Nobody knows. None of us do.

What I do know is that we are in control of our own destinies, we hold the power to conquer and climb from the holes that someone else dug for us. For some of us, the hole is so deep into the earth that water seeps in, attempting to drown before the surface is even visible, that a climb seems beyond impossible.

I am with you. I have made that slippery ascent, losing my grip at times, falling to a place below at others.

I am with you. I have squinted my eyes in attempt to foresee the end of the struggle.

I am with you. I have begged my body to carry the weight that my mind could not.

I am still climbing myself, but what has changed is my perspective and my mentality, two difficult things to alter. If not for this, my questions for tomorrow and the future beyond would be muddy and dank, just as the climb has potential for being.

So now when asked, although I cannot predict the specifics in fine details, what I can say and know is that I am ready. I am able. I see myself continue the climb, continuing to conquer. I am one to move forward, and in large strides. So that is where I see myself, tomorrow, in five years, in ten. On the move. Constant motion, always progressing.

Poetry by Emily

ODE TO AUTISM

Oh, autism.

You are my bane and my blessing,
The hoop that I must jump through,
The climb that gives me confidence.

My confidante and contender,
Battling constantly for control,
But always giving in to my fight.

You exaggerate everything and
Enhance anything and
I feel the world deeply because of it.

The sensory's of life
Are unmatched for my system
And it filters close to none.

Your grip on my movements
Cannot stop me though,
From continuing to walk my path.

Our existence is one and not two,
For you are me
And I am you.

TRAPPED

Covered in blanket and sheet
A dream whispers out of head
Leaving as quietly as it arrived
But dreamy residue is left behind.
Just enough to twist the mind
And more than enough to terrify.
No sweet dreams of cloudy visions.
No sweet sites of a sleeper's eye.
Instead creeps forth a darkness
A chill
A sense of overwhelming doom.
It moves in slowly, gently
Almost as if a welcomed friend.
Cradles a motionless body
Still wrapped in comfort of sleep
And comfort of dream
And just as sun begins to wake,
With it my eyes want to do the same.
But darkness looms, and
Panic. In body, breath and bone.
Trapped. In the vessel of my own.
Wake up. Wash the sleep away.
Trapped. Blackness turns to grey.
Wake up. Dread closing in.
Trapped. Trapped in my own skin.
Panic.
Figures they do form
In the visions of my mind.
Caught between sleep and wake.
Caught between real and fake.
And even if i wanted to,

Paralysis won't let me move.

Frozen still under sheet,

Nightmarish faces dance towards me.

Heart is racing in my throat

And terror consumes this bedroom now.

Panic.

Scream.

A breath escapes. I gasp for air.

Eyes flash open

Brightness sneaks in.

The darkness creeps away,

Leaving as quietly as it arrived,

Nightmarish residue left behind.

More than enough to tire my mind.

And now the question with which i am left;

When will i be trapped again?

PHOTOGRAPHIC MIND

The place time has frozen
Faces even remain the same
Pictures in my memory playing time the fool.
Forage through the images
Taking me by surprise
Pouring out like water
Imagination is what's real
Real life stopped, preserved in just glimpses
Hope lingers lasting
Pictures never fading.
Frozen images frozen time.

ARE YOU OKAY?

I know my name, but that wasn't your question. I can let the
syllables slip off my tongue but some may not understand.
Emily. Emily Faith Grodin to be exact.

I know what you want, understand the request. But often as not
my body will choose to do what it wants, and not what you do.

I don't know what's wrong, why don't you tell me. Perhaps the
political state, or the fact that our planet is dying. I can think of
a myriad of things, but if you're asking of me, you're asking the
wrong thing.

Oh, should I? Should I calm down? You must think I enjoy losing
control. Must think I don't want that peace too.

And oh, is that too loud? Me? Too loud? Try hearing it from
inside my own head. Try hearing life from inside my head. The
ringing phone, a passing plane, my own pounding heart, beat
beat beating away. Then you might truly know loud.

I don't know what I need, or even if I do, how do I make it
known? When I have no way to form the words. Cannot
properly plan the steps it would take to get it myself.

And here come the choices. So few choices for such a complex
human being.

How very unlikely that one of those three things is actually what I
need. Ah, but here come some more, too many more. And soon
I am swimming, drowning, in the choices you've given me.

Sure, I'll try again. I'll try again, and again, and again. Because
I want to succeed, and I comprehend the details. But when
I cannot do what you've asked, you will think that I don't
understand. What a false representation of me.

No, I'm not okay. I am struggling to say the words, fumbling over
the movements. What about this is okay?

Tell me, what about this is okay.

HEARD

People on the streets
Who need their messages to carry
Whether peaceful
Or radical
Whether silent
Or screaming.
A voice is a voice
Whether calm
Or desperate
And a message holds no meaning
Unless it is heard.

Do we hear them?
I ask you,
I ask myself.
Because I know what it's like
To not have a voice.
When I was peaceful
Or radical
If I was silent
Or screaming.
My voice was a voice
Whether calm
Or desperate
And my message held no meaning
Unless I was heard.

People on the streets.
I want their message to carry
Because humans are peaceful

Until we become radical.
When we are silenced
We scream.
Our collective voice is a voice
When we are calm,
When we are desperate.
And our message hold no meaning
Until we are heard.

TALKING SANDWICH.

Make me a sandwich
Yes, with mustard please.
Listen, I've been thinking.
Sure a pickle would be good.
Really though
We should talk.
Lettuce?
Fine.
No. No mayo, thanks.
Trying to cut some extra calories.
Please just hear me out,
There's something I should tell you,
I am going crazy keeping it inside.
I . . . what's that?
There should be some behind the milk,
Look next to the leftovers,
Yes, I agree it's not worth eating without cheese.
All sandwiches need cheese.
I'm just going to get this off my chest,
Should only take a moment.
Cut in half is fine.
Chips?
Fine.
Will you stop with the goddamn sandwich already!
I need to tell you something!
You know what?
Forget it.
No.
Lost my appetite for some reason.
Yeah . . . help yourself.

SHOELACES

Life is easy through the eyes of a child
Possibilities are not taken for as expectation
Incredible bounty of curiosity running wild
Moved only by sweet temptation

Learning each day to greet the shining of the sun
With its warmth full of rays do glisten
No thoughts of things undone
More care to the game than to the lesson

Like shoelaces double knotted
Soon to come untied
Children step into a world uncharted
Marking sure to feel their way to pride

Yes it's beauty through the eyes of a child
It is only later the world leaves us beguiled

RARE WORDS

I do not have the words to be able
To tell you what it is like in my mind.
Even though my senses are unstable
The rest of me is perfectly aligned.

My lack of words don't mean I can't convey;
For I know exactly how to describe
What I just physically cannot say
Despite how statements from brain don't transcribe.

And so I type my expressions instead
One slow letter, single words at a time
To pour them onto a screen from my head
And if I'm lucky I can make them rhyme.

It's not typical but works fine for me;
Rare girl swimming in a typical sea.

SILENT POET

Living in a world of constant noise.
Horn blares. Baby cries. Dog barks.
Alone sits a quiet poet. A silent poet.
Tap tap tap.
A silenced poet tapping through a leaf blowers song.
A quiet girl sifting through melodic words in mind.
Competing with the spoken words and rantings of a television
program better viewed if muted.
A silent poet deep in thought.
Water drips. Papers rustle. Birds screech.
A silent poem begins to breathe.
Lost to the noise if not for a gift of quiet air from its maker.
Flowing breath from herself in the form of fancy words and
    dramatic pause.
Doorbell rings. Heavy footsteps. Voices heard.
A welcomed distraction silently pulls the poet away.
The sound of an ancient door creak greets the ears of a silent
    poet.
A one way conversation entertained politely.
For guarantee of the unbroken silence that will surely follow.
Tap tap tap.
A silenced poet tapping though the song of the moons whispered
    glow.
A song so soft almost impossible to hear.
A quiet companion to a silent poet.
Bidding goodnight and sweet dreams to the constant noise.
With the only sound left to be heard. That of a silent poem.
Tap tap tap.

FOREIGN SOIL

A flood of newness which surrounds my senses,
To label them simply as sights and smells would be unjust.
For they are so different, beyond unique
From that of which I am accustomed,
So that each particle enters my system and whispers to me
That I am present in a place unknown to my experiences.
Sun that sets late and defies circadian,
And time zones that cause alarm
Only comforting to the traveler that has exhausted body and mind
When rest comes in the unslept sheets of a strangers bed.
And when morning arrives, and the city calls
With synchronized sounds of muffled pedestrians and the blare of
    foreign auto,
It tempts from sleepy dreams and warm blanket
That discovery awaits.
And a new day that asks for method of transport
By way of a flailing hand, or plastic cards, or tired soles.
And asks to be acknowledged by strange architecture and the notice of
    language not your own,
A constant reminder you are so far from home.

Oceans between point of reference and point of the destiny,
Too far to possibly carry you back on a free whim.
This unknown land that begs your acquaintance,
And speaks to you through neon signs and song unheard.
Reminds you endlessly of an empty belly
Through wafts of herbs and season that drift carelessly with you down
    stony streets,
And invite you into cozy holes to feed the appetite and quench parched
    tongue.

With menu handed by an eager tender, who decrypts the unknown
  selections to tired traveler,
Reminding you in accented word that this foreign land to them is
  home.
Which sparks a thought so foreign on its own,
To imagine a life lived on this unknown soil,
To think that these things so foreign to me
Are the comforts and acquaintance of another,
Born to these lands and these flavors, these scents,
Strange though to me, but home to the other.
And this brings visible joy to my masque, to know that this place is
  loved
In a way that only a home can be loved.

And even more strange than these lands and the languages and
  customs and sights all unique,
Is that I attempt to see my own land as the traveler would see.
And I wonder what would shock them, surprise them, impress.
What sights would overflow them, speak to them,
And marvel them as their land has done to me?
But I push this away, suppress it so that
Nothing interrupts the constant stream of this land that is not my
  own, not my home,
But has welcomed me, asked of my attention, craves so deeply that I
  never forget,
That it sends me off with trinkets and toys
With its name scribbled or inked across them.
And those items, while special and sacred in my own box,
Can do no justice, as the memories also cannot,
To fill my senses with a foreign land.

IMPOSSIBLE TO EXPLAIN

It would be a stretch
To suggest
That I could possibly describe
The experience that I live inside,
Inside this body of mine
That doesn't behave quite as tame
As the things I think inside my brain.

I wish I could tell
Just how well
I have had to teach myself
How to be
A thinking person in the world around me
Because anything else would have been easy.
I don't like easy.

And speaking of easy,
I could have just been
Content to stay quiet and watch the world spin
Without contributing a single thing
Or even speaking a single word
That meant something to anyone.
Thats what I could have done.

Its impossible to explain
Even harder to understand
The way my life has
Been a series of events all chosen by me
Despite a lack of planning my motor clearly
Or being able to speak my mind.
So instead I write mine.

It would take some time
To really convey
How different I function in every way
And how most things you do
Are different for me
My wiring built a little unique
And the sensory experience I do seek.

I have tried my best
To make my words known
To write the ways I've learned to grow
Made the effort to let people see
Deep inside the autistic mind
The inner workings of a brain refined
The being of someone who has not consigned.

So you see
Try as I might
I could write and write, yet still not quite
Tell it all and tell it true
But try I will, continue to pursue
Explaining the impossible
Until I have explained it through.

WRONG

They said I had no way to understand the world.
And that I would never know a whole life.
That I was too this and I was too that
And that I couldn't grow to be who I am.
They were wrong.
They told me to calm down, they said to relax.
But they failed to provide me with the map
That would lead me in the proper direction.
They were wrong.
So I wrote the map myself
And despite their lack of help
I found the way to go without asking anybody else.
Because when they were wrong
Little did they know
That I would be determined to help myself grow.
I would figure out the way
Find my own straight path
And once my own was written I'd help others write their map.
They'll see they were wrong
To think so small of me
To assume that I'd be any less than the person that is me.
I think maybe if I'm honest
I should have thanked them all along.
I am everything I am today because
They were wrong.

Acknowledgments

There is no question that Emily was the direct beneficiary of the federal and state laws that mandated the delivery of services and opportunities to those with disabilities in the public school. Had it not been for tireless advocates who demanded the changes and the political leaders who agreed, Emily would not have had the opportunities and choices she did. While access to what Emily was entitled to did not come without the initial guidance of Valerie Vanaman, Esq., a true advocate for those with special needs, and the ongoing vigilance by me and Tom, the fact is that the law was on our side. We were lucky that the 1990s and the early 2000s were truly the heyday of opportunity for services, at least in our district. The constellation of services that she received, and not one single one or the other, most definitely fostered growth in Emily and got her to where we are today.

Since Emily's diagnosis in 1993 the number of children diagnosed with autism has increased exponentially. There is a real need to acknowledge that for those on the spectrum who are minimally speaking or nonverbal, traditional speech therapy is not always the answer to solving the problem of communication. It is time to recognize that all forms of AAC including FC must be considered legitimate methods. We are hopeful that our story, and that of so many others whose lives have been changed through FC, will result in the inclusion of FC as a viable and useful tool on the road to improving communication for those who would otherwise be left out of the conversation.

We would like to thank the incredible Michael Palgon, who believed in our story early on, championed it, and knew it was one that the world should hear and worked tirelessly to shepherd it to fruition, and Rabbi Sherre Hirsch, who introduced us. Thank you to Bernadette Murphy for being a friend, adviser, and literary guide in this process. We would also like to thank our wonderful editors at William Morrow, Mauro DiPreta and Vedika Khanna, for their insight and care with this manuscript. Thank you to Darlene Hanson for being the early beacon of light who made us aware of FC and promoted it, and provided guidance to us and so many others in accessing it, as well as to Lindsey Goodrich, a gifted communication partner, whom we loved from the very first moment we met her and who always believed in what was possible for Emily. Thank you to Stephanie Lewis, who continued to carry Emily on the journey, to Nik Jayaram, who inspired so much in Emily, and to Marta Amaya, who has been with us through the good, the bad, and the awful.

Lastly, to Tom, who never wavered in his love for us despite all our challenges: thank you, loving husband and father, for being our rock, our source of comfort and caring—that is, for everything.

Note from the Authors

All italicized text is original to Emily and has not been edited by anyone including the publisher of this book. All of Emily's work is first draft.

Emily works with many different facilitators. All of them use the same methodology of touching the shoulder of her shirt and no part of her body.

Emily uses an iPad which typically sits on a stand on a desk or table.

Authenticity of the work can be found in Emily's recollection of childhood and family events and personal experiences, all of which were unknown to any facilitator.